A Beginners Guide - An Introduction to Criminology

A Plain English Guide to Criminology

CW01497526

By Teresa Clyne MSc

"Justice will be realised only when people are willing to obey the unenforceable." **Socrates**

"Dedicated to all of those who change the lives of others by empowering them for greatness."

This book is written "as is", it is compiled in very basic introductory or note form, it is similar to the notes you would receive in a lecture, and the author then compiles these notes and hand-outs into an easy to use booklet. It is, where possible, compiled in spoken English, pretty much as you would chat with your friends over coffee, it is meant for those who wish to learn this fascinating subject in plain ordinary spoken words. (with legal and medical/psychological terminology thrown in) If you are looking for a grammatically perfect and Queens English book for your learning or information, <u>then this is not it</u>. I write as I speak. N.B this criminology book also deals with legal systems, and it concentrates on the **Irish legal system**, *with <u>outlines</u> from the legal systems of England & Wales.*

Disclaimer:

No liability is accepted by Teresa M Clyne BA, MSc for any action taken or not taken in reliance on the information set out in this publication. Any and all information is subject to change and professional or legal advice should be obtained before taking or refraining from any action as a result of the contents of this publication. This booklet is written in spoken English, and is intended to help lay (non-legal) persons who want to understand the basics of Criminology.

*This is **not** an academic textbook; it is a very basic foot in the door of this amazing world of crime, criminals and the authorities that deal with the them, however, some beginners may find it helps them in the early stages of their studies or those taking introductory courses in Criminology.*

Table of Contents

Criminological Theories

Introduction

This introductory booklet focuses on the vital core of criminological theories; such as, theory, method, and criminal behaviour. Each chapter is written in a plain way, which is has at its centre, spoken English for ease of reading, but also, comprehension. This is to make sure it is straightforward, and will enable readers to more fully comprehend this difficult subject.

It covers current topics, along with historical principles and theories; these principles and theories are explored to give the reader the basis to understand not only the core of criminology, but to form an unbiased subjective opinion on where criminology has come from, equally important, where it is going. No one viewpoint is dominant in Criminology.

Many theories are used when attempting to define crime, with stark differences between the "mainstream" theories and "critical" theories. Criminology is the study of crime; a "crime" is the commission (doing) of an act or omissions (failing to do) which is illegal. The state will punish wrongdoers.

Criminology also asks why do certain people commit crimes, what is the reason for it, why does race, gender or age have an impact on criminal behaviour? It also asks what impact crime has on society and, the reactions of society to them.

Some of the questions criminologists ask and answers sought in criminology research include;

1.   Why do crime rates vary from time to time and from culture to culture?
2.   Why are some people more prone to committing crime than others?
3.   Why do crime rates vary across different ages, genders, and racial/ethnic groups?
4.   Why are some detrimental acts criminalised and not others?
5.   What can society do to prevent crime?

The two main theories of criminology;

Biological Theories

•   Criminal are "born"

Sociological Theories

•   Criminals are "made"

Conventional theorists focus on predefined, set crimes, these theorists explain crimes principally in terms of individual traits, but also, features of the immediate social environment, particularly the family, school, peer, work, and neighbourhood environments. Critical theorists, on the other hand use broader definitions of crime, these theorists predominately focus on corporate and state crimes, they explain such crimes in terms of the general social environment, particularly conflict between the rich and poor, also social divides within society.

Criminologists believed there were several policies for controlling crime, including deterrence (sanctions or fines severe enough to deter offending), incapacitation, (removing offenders from society so they cannot commit crimes), "imprisonment", and rehabilitation and prevention (educating and establishing ways to cut crime from happening in the first place).

This guide also looks at the effects crime has on society and policy decisions, and the connection between theory and criminal behaviour.

Chapter One

What is Criminology all about?

Criminology, is a relatively young discipline, however, the theories of crime, of rules and who breaks them, and why, are as old as man himself. In the early days, as you will read in the coming chapters, crime and criminal behaviours were thought to have been caused by some spiritual or religious force, such as being possessed by demons or spiritual forces taking over the free will of the person.

Sin was a major contributor of social control, those who sinned in specific ways would not enter the kingdom of heaven, and this alone was enough to keep some people on the straight and narrow, the religious establishments claimed those who sinned had veered from God's path.

Other non-religious thinkers were more concerned about an offender's physical appearance, than that of their relationship with God. For instance, Shakespeare's Julius Caesar distrusted Cassius because; he "has a lean and hungry look." These appearance trait diagnoses were used by the Italian physician, named Giambattista della Porta, who developed a theory of human personality called physiognomy, in 1558.

Porta claimed that the study of physical appearance, particularly of the face, could show much about a person's personality and character.

Thieves, for instance, he claimed, have large lips and sharp vision. Porta was writing during an historical period known as, the Renaissance, a period between approximately 1450 and 1600. This period saw a change in thinking from the pure God-centred supernaturalism, and relative barbarism of the Middle Ages, to more human-centred naturalism. The Enlightenment was the period approximately between 1650 and 1800. It might be said that, the Renaissance provided a key to the human mind, and the Enlightenment opened the door. The Enlightenment era in history is associated with not only advances in mathematics, and science, but also, the dignity and worth of the individual, as demonstrated by a concern for human rights. This concern led to reforms in criminal justice systems throughout Europe, a process driven by the work of Cesare Beccaria. His book **On Crimes and Punishments** aligned with the classical school. The classical school theorised that human rationality and free will were the causes of criminal behaviour, which was heavily influenced by Charles Darwin's work on the evolution of species.

Theories of character, such as Franz Josef Gall's system of phrenology...assessing character from physical features of the skull...thrived. The basic idea behind phrenology was that cognitive functions are localised in the brain, and that the parts regulating the most dominant functions were bigger than parts regulating the less dominant ones.

Criminals were said to have large protuberances (bumps, lumps or growths) in parts of the brain thought to regulate craftiness, brutishness, moral insensibility, and small bumps in such "localities" as intelligence, honour, and piety (devotion). The biggest impact during this period, however, was made by Cesare Lombroso's theory of atavism, or the born criminal. Criminologists from this point on were obsessed with measuring, sorting, and sifting all kinds of data (mostly physical) about criminal behaviour.

Criminology Defined

If behaviour is caused by what people experience in their environments, so the optimistic argument went, then we can change their behaviour by changing their environment. It was during this period that sociology became the disciplinary home of criminology. Criminology became less interested in why individuals commit crime from biological or psychological points of view, and more concerned with aggregate (everything together) level, such as (social structures, neighbourhoods, subcultures, etc.) data.

It was during this period that the so-called structural theories of crime came about, such as the Chicago school of social ecology. Anomie strain theory was another structural/ cultural theory that emerged somewhat later (1938). This theory was doubtlessly influenced strongly by the American experience of the Great Depression and of the exclusion of blacks from many areas of American society.

The period from the 1950s through the early 1970s saw considerable dissatisfaction with the strong structural approach, which many viewed as proceeding as if individuals were almost irrelevant to explaining criminal behaviour. Criminological theory moved toward integrating psychology and sociology during this period and strongly emphasised the importance of socialisation.

This time was leading to the modern criminological theories of bio criminology.

Criminology Defined

Crime

The most often-quoted definition of crime is that of Merriam-Webster as:

"An act or the commission of an act that is forbidden or the omission of a duty that is commanded by a public law and that makes the offender liable to punishment by that law; especially: a gross violation of law."[1]

Criminology

Before we explain what criminology is, we will first define what criminology is NOT. It is not the criminal justice system, how the laws are made, how the Police or Gardaí work, it is not about prisoners and it is not about morals. Criminology is not about how the world should be, criminology is about the study of crime, what causes crime, why do individuals commit crimes, why do individuals commit crimes at certain times, this guide will also look at the social reaction to crime, and how this affects individuals who commit crimes.

Criminology is a branch of Sociology, criminology and sociology is sciences. "Scientia" is a Latin word for knowledge, criminology is in the "ology" field, ology is the study of something, therefore "crime" "ology" is the study of crime.

This booklet encourages you to look at the evidence, question everything you read, even what I have written, question the systems and acts, such as Mala Se and Mala Probibita crimes. "A criminologist will attempt to examine and explain criminal behaviours; they ask such questions as, why some people commit crime and others don't?

---

[1] http://www.merriam-webster.com/dictionary/crime

Criminology Defined

A criminologist will examine such things as;

- the types of crimes committed in that society or location
- the rates of crime of crime within that society or location
- what are the different crime rates in different countries, and
- how has crime evolved over time

Criminology is a social science (unlike physics, or chemistry which is natural sciences); it is concerned with making the law, breaking the law and the consequences of breaking the law, i.e. punishment.

Crimes can be categorised into two distinct fields,

"Mala in Se", these are crimes which violate society's rules, these are universal, they are obviously wrong, they are wrong or evil acts which are recognised as bad, children are told at an early age not to steal, assault or murder, etc., where they live is not important, these are moral as well as legal wrongs, therefore Mala in Se.

"Mala Prohibita" is a legal wrong, it can be more difficult to recognise, such as rules from one country to another, for instance, traffic rules may not be the same in one country as it is in another, and easier to breach. These can be such things as drunk and disorderly or not having a TV licence or not paying water rates, society may not see them as crimes but nonetheless they are.

Which of the following ten acts do you consider mala in se crimes, mala prohibita crimes, or not a crime at all? Explain each one.

- possession
- vandalism
- drink driving
- sale of alcohol to minors
- fraud
- spousal abuse
- adult male / female having consensual sex with underage person

- prostitution
- speeding

Criminology is the study of crime, however, there is also a discipline called penology, which is the study of punishment, there is a chapter later in the guide dealing with penology, this is concerned with motivation for punishment, i.e.

- Retribution (punishment for punishment's sake, people feel safer when an offender is punished)
- Rehabilitation (assisting criminals to change their ways, modern criminology and penology is looking towards rehabilitation rather than retribution in order to reduce prison numbers)
- Deterrence (put them off offending again, can you name a type of deterrence?)

Criminology is a multi-disciplinary (it deals with so many different areas and topics); it has elements of psychology, sociology, medicine, law, geography and architecture. One question I ask you before we define crime further is to ask you, have you ever committed a crime?

Have you partaken in any of the following?

- On your mobile phone while driving;
- Speeding;
- Parking without paying fees;
- Not putting tax on your car by the required date;
- Not buying your TV licence;
- Not paying your property tax

The list can go on, but there are few amongst us that can truly say they have never broken the law, (I have met one or two) I can however, put your mind at rest, let me explain, the crimes above are what I call "socially acceptable crimes, or socially acceptable criminal behaviour"

How often are you horrified that your friend got a speeding ticket or parking ticket? It is unlikely you would be, however, should they come into your home and tell you they have hit someone or knocked them down with their car, and didn't bother to stop, your acceptability of their criminal behaviour would stop here, wouldn't it?

Can you identify when criminal behaviour stops being socially acceptable?

It could be said that "if there is no law then there is no crime"

Criminology Defined

Antisocial, deviant and immoral conduct

Anti-social Behaviour

(Ireland) Section 1 of the Housing (Miscellaneous Provisions) Act, 1997 defines "anti-social behaviour" as;

b) any behaviour which causes or is likely to cause any significant or persistent danger, injury, damage, alarm, loss or fear to any person living, working or otherwise lawfully in or in the vicinity of a house provided by a housing authority under the Housing Acts 1966 to 2002 or Part V of the Planning and Development Act 2000, or a housing estate in which the house is situated or a site and, without prejudice to the foregoing.[2]

Deviance

Deviant behaviour is literally any conduct that differs from the prevailing norms of a specified group within society. (Acting or behaving outside what society believes is right) A deviant will go outside society's norms, for instance, if there is a walk on the left rule in school and they walk on the right just because they do not like rules, this can be classed as deviant, or facial tattoos or purple/ pink spiked hair, these are all examples of deviant behaviour. (However, this is relative, i.e. it may be deviant in one society and yet not another).

Immoral and Illegal behaviour

Morals: A set of rules of correct conduct inside society, breach of these rules can result in social sanctions, shunning etc.

Laws: These are rules which are enforced within society; breaches of these rules can result in criminal sanctions, fines or loss of liberty.

---

[2] Anti-Social Behaviour – Symptoms, Solutions, Strategies. Dr. Padraic Kenna, School of Law, National University of Ireland Galway.

Criminology Defined

Let us define what is meant by illegal and immoral behaviour. For example, murder and rape are immoral and illegal, (example: to take a life is immoral, but it is also illegal as it carries a criminal sanction.)

Not all immoral acts are illegal.

- Lying
- Cheating

Not all illegal acts are immoral.

- Drink driving
- Cheating on taxes
- Smoking marijuana

We can also say that some behaviour is immoral but not illegal.

For instance, in the UK and Ireland, it is not a legal requirement to save the life of a stranger. If a person was walking on the beach, and a swimmer got into difficulty there is no obligation on them to even attempt to save the life of the swimmer in difficulty, they can drown, the passer-by has not breached any law; however, society's morals would dictate that those actions were immoral and wrong. Sigmund Freud believed that all humans have criminal tendencies; he stated that criminals are made. It is through socialisation that these tendencies are controlled during childhood.

The History of Criminology

The Salem Witch Trials

The Salem Witch Trials lasted from June of 1692 to September of 1692 in Salem, which is now called, Danvers Massachusetts. The trials began when 11 year old Abigail Williams and 9 year old Elizabeth Parris began acting in an unusual manner, the Puritan ministers at the time were worried about their behaviour, singing and talking "in tongues", the ministers asked the girls if someone had cast a spell on them which they replied yes, both girls named three local women as the ones who had cast spells on them.

The three were named as; Tituba, a slave. Sarah Good, a homeless woman and, Sarah Osborne a woman who had married her servant. Over 150 people were accused of witchcraft in Salem, 24 people were hanged in the months that followed.

Profile of a witch

Used to identify witches in Europe from 1400's to 1700's:

- Elderly female beyond child bearing range
- Poor
- Lives on edge of town
- Displays knowledge of herbal medicines
- Mark of the Devil (insensitive spot)
- Steals men's potency, causing impotence in the surrounding areas
- Collects a great number of male members and keeps them in a birds nest or box[3]

Precise descriptions of witches, devils, or murderers found in *The Malleus Maleficarum* are telling of the Investigators' profiling methods and reasoning, which are entirely faith based. Some examples of profiling include the following:

- Witches have the power make men impotent and unable to copulate (p. 4):
- Witches use spells, images, and charms (p. 13):
- Witches cannot bear children (p. 23):

With respect to murder, *The Malleus Maleficarum* explains that dead bodies will flow blood from their wounds when their murderer is near. Of course this kind of profile was entirely faith based, based on fear or hysterical, it can be defined as unreliable and illogical by today's standards.

---

[3] Cyriax, 1993; Kramer & Sprenger, 1971; Ruiz, 2004

There were various tests used by the inquisitor in order to determine if an accused was a witch. These tests included:

Pressing

This test involved placing boards on the victim, then placing heavy stones on the boards, one at a time, until the accused either confessed or died.

The Sink Test

The accused was placed in a body of water, stones were tied from them, if they sank, and they were declared innocent. If they floated, they were declared a witch, and were then hanged.

The Scales Test

The accused was weighted against a metal bound bible, if they were lighter than the Bible; they were found guilty and declared a witch. If they were heavier than the Bible, scales, they were declared innocent.

Satan's Mark

The local minister would check the accused body for Satan's marks, usually black but, some of those marks were only visible to the minister, upon finding the marks the minister would poke the mark with needles, if it bled or was sore they were innocent, if they felt no pain they were witches.

The Prayer Test

Unless the accused could recite the Lord's Prayer flawlessly they were declared a witch, even a stammer defined it as flawed and declared a witch.

The Dunk Test

This test involved the accused being tied to a chair, and then thrown into a body of water, if they sank they were innocent, if the floated they were taken out and declared guilty and hanged.

Pre-Enlightenment Europe

Law at this time was violent and terrifying for those who sought to rely on it, when often times the victims were punished for making a complaint and even the smallest complaint could find a person thrown in prison awaiting trial. A trial which could take years or in fact never happen at all, offenders could be found guilty and sentenced to death with little or no proof of guilt.

Judges were given unfettered powers and offenders were often sentenced for crimes which were never in fact defined as crimes, there was no legal or formal processes or procedures in court and no legal representations were allowed to the persons accused who were normally tortured in order to obtain confessions and admit guilt,

Once the offender was found guilty the punishments were severe and swift, usually much more severe for the poor than sentences or punishments for the rich who could easily buy themselves out of trouble and even be exempt from any kind of punishments.

Crime in the Middle-Ages was associated with religion and demonic manipulation. In short, the best way to explain crime was the influence the devil had on society or an individual. Besides crime, natural disasters were the work of demons.

The bubonic plague (Black Death) which swept through Europe, the UK and Ireland in the 1300's leaving countless dead bodies in its wake was an example of demonic influences at work. During this era, deviant acts were considered to be a sin requiring harsh punishment or death. Some of the medieval ordeals which the accused had to endure in these times were as follows:

Medieval Trials

Trial by Ordeal

Judicium Dei (Judgment of God) or God will help the innocent.

Trial by Ordeal was used in Europe until 1220. (This was later replaced by trial by jury). It was used to determine the guilt or innocence of an accused person. The innocent person completed the task uninjured or their wounds would heal properly. The guilty would suffer injury or their wounds would fester.

Trial by Fire

The defendant (accused) must walk across hot coals to retrieve an object; if they successfully get to the other side unscathed then they are innocent.

(Even if they got burnt, their wounds should heal quickly, "within days"), if it festered then they are guilty and could be sentenced to be hung, drawn or quartered.

Trial by Water

The defendant was bound in the foetal position and thrown into the water. The priest was the judge and there was the pomp and ceremony involved.

[4]As in the public executions of the 16th Century, those that sank weren't drowned, but were hauled out of the water; if he or she floated, they were guilty, and if they sank, they were presumed innocent.

---

[4] Ordeal of boiling water, illustration from a 14th century manuscript, (public domain image via Wikimedia Commons

Trial by Water (varying countries)

Casting the accused into water with a millstone around his/her neck – the innocent would not sink, (the weight of the crime did not press upon the innocent). Therefore the innocent were released, the guilty were removed just before they were tortured and killed.

Hanged, drawn and quartered

The process began with the prisoner being placed on a wooden frame and dragged through the streets to the place of execution. On arrival they would be placed on the gallows and hung until close to death.

Now comes the not so nice part. Whilst still alive, they would be cut open and disembowelled, and to add insult to injury, they would often have their private parts cut off and then be beheaded.

Trial by Hot Water

The accused would have to put their arm elbow-deep into hot water, to grasp a ring, stone, or holy object at the bottom of a pot. After several days, if no blistering or peeling was present, the defendant was presumed innocent.

Example of other Ordeals (from around the world)

Internationally, there are such trials as, trial of "Old Calabar" (Ordeal bean) a poisonous bean, if ingested by the innocent they would survive, if guilt they would die.

This particular ordeal was the favourite ordeal when a person was accused of witchcraft.

Wooden stocks/pillory

The stocks and pillory was a form of public punishment, public humiliation. **Stocks** were wooden or metal devices with foot holes. The convict was seated and had their feet and ankles locked into the device so that the legs were held out straight. A **pillory** was also a wooden or metal device with holes to lock the convicted individual's head and hands in place. It was impossible to sit while in a pillory.

All of the local shops and businesses in the area would shut down while the convicts were paraded through the streets, as I said; this punishment was to humiliate the guilty party and have their faces known in the locality. Once the parade was done, the convict was then strapped into the pillory or stock in the street, where locals could throw mud, dirt and rotten food at them.

For the final insult to injury, all of the locals would parade up and down past the convict calling them names and even spitting on them.

Cangue

In china there was varying ordeals but the one that survived until modern times, the defendant was shut into a cangue, the crimes they were accused of were put on a scroll on the end, they could not eat or drink themselves, if the people around them believed they were guilty, then they were not fed or given water, (therefore guilty and would die) this is thought to be the first form of trial by jury.[5]

---

[5] William Alexander [Public domain]

The Death of Medieval Trials

In 1220, trial by ordeal was abolished and trial by Panel was introduced. This created a new system called trial by panel. Under this principle, a group of prominent men would listen to the testimony and look at the evidence and then pronounce guilt or innocence. From this system of trial by panel we got our own system of trial by jury.

This was brought into being to give effect to natural justice, (fair, just and right). It is the ancient ancestor of our modern common law system. A jury of twelve free men was assigned to arbitrate in these disputes. Unlike the modern jury, these men were charged with uncovering the facts of the case on their own rather than listening to arguments in court.

In the 1600 compurgation was introduced (12 men who investigated the case were replaced with the pre modern 12 peers (peers also removed, now 12 persons).

In the 1700s the idea of prisons was made popular by religious orders, religious orders believed that if a person was put into a small confined room with a bible for a specific length of time they would be reborn and no longer commit crimes.

From the mid-1800s the modern criminal justice systems uses Judge and Jury. The prosecution (the State) would present their case and the defence (person accused) would present theirs. The jury would then look at the facts and decide the guilt or innocence of the defendant.

The Enlightenment Age

The Enlightenment age

This period marked a departure from the old religious description of the world and a more scientific explanation was developed. Theorists opposed cruel punishments by introducing reason and science into society. They challenged ideas which were grounded in religion and superstition. This time saw the introduction of the social contract; this contract was based on the right to govern by consent of the people rather than the divine consent of the church or royalty.

The social contract basically stated that citizens are required to give up some of their freedoms to do as they please in return for a structured Police force and laws that protect everyone. The needs and rights of the many outweigh the needs of the few (Utilitarianism).

It was at this time that the Rule of Law, rather than by theology was introduced. It was in this age that some astute judges began to remove some crimes from the throws of the guillotine or noose, for such crimes as petty theft or affray (public disorder), one particular case in 1770 whereby a mother was sentenced to death for theft.

Mary Jones was hanged as a direct consequence of the law in the UK at that time, the law stated the government could press gang any person into service on the ships, Mary's husband was removed from the family home leaving Mary without income to support her children, she was made homeless and ended up on the streets with her children, she stole some material from a clothes shop and was caught, she was sentenced to death. Her death created such uproar that more and more judges became aware of the need to differentiate crimes and seek alternative sentences.

It was at this time in the mid-1700s that some people working in State positions and power began to question the mode and methods of crime was dealt with, the slow introduction of police dealing with and preventing crime rather than the swift execution of law breakers was welcomed and the pubic hangings which many viewed as a weekly outing were condemned by Peace keeper (Justice of the Peace) Henry Fielding. Watchmen were set up; these watchmen were the precursor to the Police force, the first Police in the UK was made up of the Henry Fielding's Bow Street Runners and in Ireland by John de Blaquire (Watchmen) with the formation of both Police forces after this time by virtue of Wellesley's.

Dublin Metropolitan Police Act (1808)

Sir Robert Peel was the home secretary who introduced in a series of acts to establish a central Police force; this took some time to establish, but the Metropolitan Police Act in 1829 established Britain's (and Ireland's Irish Constabulary Act (1836)) first professional police force, under the control of two police commissioners who were responsible directly to Robert Peel.

The force was initially established at 3,000 men, many recruited from existing Bow Street Runners and also from ex members of the army. Peel was an advocate for change and repealed the death penalty for larceny in shops (Mary Jones) and on board ships; in fact he gave the judges powers to refuse the death penalty for all crimes except murder, reducing the amount of executions immediately.

After Robert Peel became Prime Minister in 1835 the use of Gibbetting (or hanging dead bodies or body parts for public display) and Pillory (stocks) was abolished. Peel believed that there would be no reform in the criminal law until the Police were reformed and that crime rates would reduce when the Police lead by example not execution, the reform of the Police finally started when all counties in the Country were required to conform to a set of specific rules, laid out in the County and Borough Police Act of 1856.

This led to the modern judicial system, criminology, a branch of sociology (why people do what they do) which has its modern roots in classicism and positivism, which began in the late 1800's. It took some 40 years for the death penalty to be removed by all judges and some continued to order the death penalty for menial crimes and the last recorded child to fall victim to the gallows was a nine-year-old boy from Essex who was found guilty of arson. According to classical criminology, humans are logical and behave in accordance with free will and rational choice. The motivation for deviant behaviour is the pursuit of pleasure (hedonistic) while avoiding pain.

This led to the belief that in order to deter crime, the pain of punishment must outweigh any pleasure that may be gained. This principle highlighted that the criminal justice system failed to consider how personal circumstances influenced an offender's criminal behaviour.

Chapter two – Theorists & Schools of Thought – The Old School

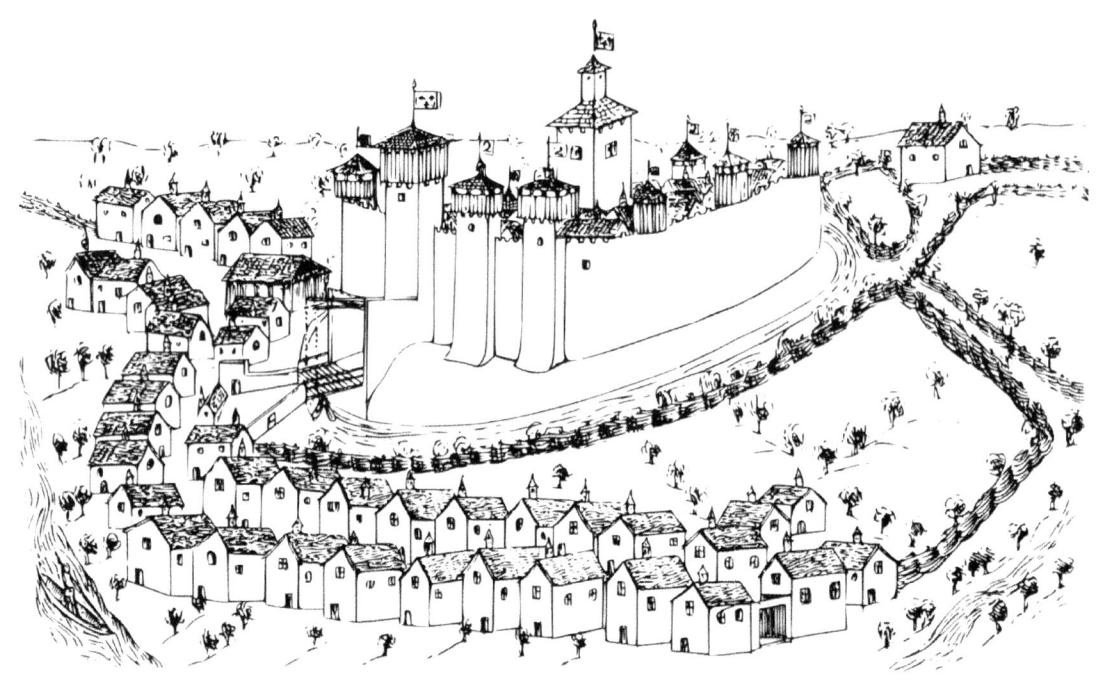

The Classical School

The Classical theory was developed in response to the corrupt, arbitrary, and harsh systems of criminal justice that existed in Europe during the 1700s. These laws were often vague, with the bribery of judge's commonplace, and punishments for the same crime varied widely between offenders depending on tier class or ethnicity, punishments were often quite harsh, involving torture and death.

This is when the Classical theory wanted to replace this system with one that was more fair and just. They claimed that people are rational and pursued their own interests, in order to maximise their pleasure and minimise their pain.

People choose to engage in crime when they believed that the proceeds of the crime will bring more pleasure than pain of any punishment, the classical theorists contended that the best way to control crime is to ensure that the pain of punishment outweighs the pleasure of crime, but only if the punishment was swift, severe and certain, meaning that all laws should be the same for everyone and punishment fitted the crimes. Classic criminology began with the view that human behaviour was rational; it claimed that people have the ability to choose right from wrong. Cesare Beccaria and Jeremy Betham who were concerned about the criminal justice system and its shortcomings were the advocates in the Classical School. Classicism believed that criminality and the administration of criminal justice were based on principles of rationality, choice, responsibility, and the deterrent power of punishment. (Beccaria).

The roots of rational choice theory go all the ways back to these classical theorists, the central points of their theory are:

1. Rationality involves an end/means calculation,

2. People (freely) choose behaviour, both conforming and deviant, based on their rational calculations

3. The central element of calculation involves a cost benefit analysis: Pleasure versus Pain [hedonistic]

4. Choice, with all other conditions equal, will be directed towards the maximization of individual pleasure,

5. The choice can be controlled through the perception and understanding of the potential pain or punishment that will follow an act judged to be in violation of the social good, the social contract,

6. The state is responsible for maintaining order and preserving the common good through a system of laws (this system is the embodiment of the social contract),

7. The Swiftness, Severity, and Certainty of punishment are the key elements in understanding a law's ability to control human behaviour. (Keel, R. 1997)

This went against the former belief that deviant behaviour was attributed to heredity or demonic possession. Beccaria and Bentham also advocated for less cruel forms of punishment.

Cesare Beccaria (1738–94)

Cesare Beccaria focused on 18th-century law; he was an advocate of the social contract theory (these were the legal protections people had to against crime, they gave up certain freedoms in return for state protection.), he believed in guilt and punishment, this punishment was for the want of pleasure and pain was the purpose of punishment.

The purpose of punishment is to prevent a criminal from doing any further injury to the community and to prevent others from committing similar crimes. Cesare Beccaria was born on March 15, 1738, and died in 1794. Beccaria believed that punishment in the 1700s was barbaric, inhumane and unjust. He believed that each individual possessed free will and could choose whether or not to commit crimes, however, he also believed that they were easily manipulated. Classical theory suggests that humans look out for themselves first, even if that means committing illegal or immoral acts, Beccaria stated that due to the need to look after the self-first offenders could be controlled and also predictable.

Beccaria stated that the purpose of the criminal justice system was to control deviant behaviour, to ensure that the punishment fits the crime; he also suggested that the aim of the just system should be that of deterrence rather than punishment. He was an advocate of the social contract, and breaches of that contract showed that the offender was aware of their actions and the consequences of breaching social responsibility. Beccaria advocated a fair and just punishment for breaching any social contracts.

In defining Beccaria and his theories, it can be stated that his views were that;

- Human behaviour as essentially rational
- Humans possessed the ability to choose right from wrong;
- They weigh up the consequences and then decide whether to commit the crime or not.
- A person's choice to breach the law was due to the desire to obtain pleasure and avoid pain.

Therefore, classical schools stated that any sentence that would be imposed should be enough to ensure that the pain of the sentence was severe enough to deter the behaviour. Beccaria, (who wrote; On Crimes and Punishment, in 1764 which started as a college essay) believed that the general public was in favour of the social contract and that most were in favour of the abolishment of the death penalty.

Beccaria believed:

- that a person could be influenced in their decision-making and influence those to commit crimes or not to.
- education of the population in the law and consequences of breaching them.
- believed that citizens would be happy to give up some of their freedoms "so that (they) might enjoy the rest of it in peace and safety".[6]

---

[6] http://major-prepa.com/wp-content/uploads/2017/05/shutterstock_445154257.jpg

Jeremy Bentham

Bentham was the forefather of Utilitarianism; this is the doctrine that the purpose of all actions should be to bring about the greatest happiness for the greatest number of people.

He also coined the phrase Felicitous calculus, this is a moral calculus for estimating the probability that a person will engage in a particular kind of behaviour.

Jeremy Bentham was a British philosopher, born in 1748. Like Beccaria he believed that people have the ability to choose right from wrong. His explanation for criminal behaviour included the idea that people are basically hedonistic (seek pleasure), that is, they desire a high degree of pleasure and avoid pain. He wrote the now famous Introduction to the Principles of Morals and Legislation which was written in 1780.

He believed that the pain of punishment should be in excess to the pleasure received when the crime is committed. Bentham was also in favour of the prison system, and wrote extensively about prison design and management. He is also known for his invention of the idea of the "panopticon", (a circular prison with cells arranged around a central well, from which prisoners could at all times be observed)[7]

---

[7] https://en.wikipedia.org/wiki/Panopticon

Beccaria was the father of the concept of Utilitarianism; this is a principle that all actions should be to bring about the greatest happiness for the greatest number of people. He stated that punishment was a necessary evil, but necessary it was, in order to stop even greater evils being committed upon society. Beccaria's and Bentham's theories argued that the proper objective of punishment should be to protect society and its laws. They both agreed that punishment should not be inflicted for revenge; instead, the primary purpose of punishment should be the reduction or deterrence of crime.

In a nutshell: *The Classical theory believed that the punishments inflicted should be just severe enough to outweigh any pleasures, to deter crime in future.*

Neoclassical

Neoclassical theory used the classical theory, but expanded it so that it also included the theory that there are certain factors, such as insanity which might inhibit the exercise of free will. This combination of the classical theory of free will, hedonistic pleasures seeking and responsibility of each individual, together with considerations of age, mental state and mitigating circumstances gave birth to what is often referred to as the Neoclassical Theory of Crime.

This system was the foundation for the modern criminal justice systems which are now used in most countries in the world. Neoclassical theories of crime are rooted in the classical school. The development of the neoclassical school.

- In the late 1800s, classical criminology gave way to the approach known as positivism
- Positivism uses the scientific method to study criminality
- Positivism is based on hard determinism, the belief that crime results from forces beyond one's control, and rejects the idea of free will

- Places greater emphasis on rationality and cognition than classical criminologist

Examples:

- **Routine activity theory:** this theory requires three elements; a motivated offender with the intention to commit a crime, the ability to act on these intentions with a suitable victim or target, the absence of a capable guardian who can prevent the crime from happening. All three must be present at the same time to define a crime. (more on page 49)
- **Rational choice theory:** Rational choice theory states that people freely choose their behaviour and are motivated by the avoidance of pain and the pursuit of pleasure. (pleasure v. pain theory) (more on page 64).
- Rational choice theory assumes a criminally motivated offender and focuses on the process of the choice to offend. Choice structuring: The offender will process the plain versus gain before committing any crime. i.e. they will weigh up the penalties for getting caught, if they get caught as to the pleasure the criminal act will bring them.
- Deterrence: The prevention of criminal acts by the use or threat of punishment. Specific deterrence refers to the effect of punishment on the future behaviour of the person who experiences the punishment.
- Recidivism: (Reoffending), it's a known statistic that 88% of inmates in Mountjoy prison at any one time are reoffenders.

Cesare Lombroso

Lombroso was one of the first theorists who attempted to scientifically study criminal behaviour; he believed that physical stigmata, such as a long lower jaw, flattened nose, and long, apelike arms, identify a criminal. These biological characteristics were seen as atavism, or a throwback to earlier stages in human evolution.

Lombroso in 1876 argued that the criminal is a separate species between modern and primitive humans, physical shape of the head and face determined the "born criminal" - primitive and were unable to adapt to modern morality.

Cesare Lombroso and William Sheldon's interpretation of Criminals, and examples of criminal types.

Lombroso in 1876 argued that the criminal is a separate species between modern and primitive humans. He claimed that the physical shape of the head and face determined the "born criminal" - primitive and were unable to adapt to modern morality.

These people were primitive and were unable to adapt to modern morality. His view was based on genetics. The atavist (primitive genetic form) and had large jaws, high cheek bones, large ears, extra nipples, toes or fingers, and were insensitive to pain.

Therefore, murderers were said to have:

•   Cold, glassy, bloodshot eyes, curly, abundant hair, strong jaws, long ears and thin lips

Whilst sex offenders have:

•   Glinting eyes, strong jaws, thick lips, lots of hair and projecting ears.'

Lombroso went further and suggested that from the surveys he had carried out in prison, he could detect physiological differences between different types of criminal.

In his book, ***Criminal Man (1876***), Lombroso claimed that nature vs. nurture was easily defined, and he claimed that nature was the culprit in crime, and not nurture. (How you are brought up is irrelevant, it was your genes that decided who you were and how you behaved). However, modern criminology can debunk this theory due to research and evidence showing how nurture (how they were brought up) can outweigh nature (predisposed from birth) in many criminals.

William Sheldon

Sheldon was an American psychologist and numismatist. He was the creator of somatotype plus constitutional psychology, this field attempted to correlate body types with behaviour, this included intelligence and social hierarchy.

William Sheldon believed that people could be classified into three body shapes, which correspond with three different personality types.[8]

• Endomorphic (fat and soft) tend to be sociable and relaxed.

• Ectomorphics (thin and fragile) are introverted and restrained

• Mesomorphic (muscular and hard) tend to be aggressive and adventurous.

Sheldon, using a correlational study, found that many convicts were mesomorphic, and they were least likely to be ectomorphic (Sheldon et al 1949). This has since been attributed to the fact that mesomorphics were large and noticeable, and if they were seen at a crime scene they would be remembered easier.

---

[8] Richard N. Walker (1978). "W. H. Sheldon" (PDF). Nature journal in Psychiatric

William Sheldon

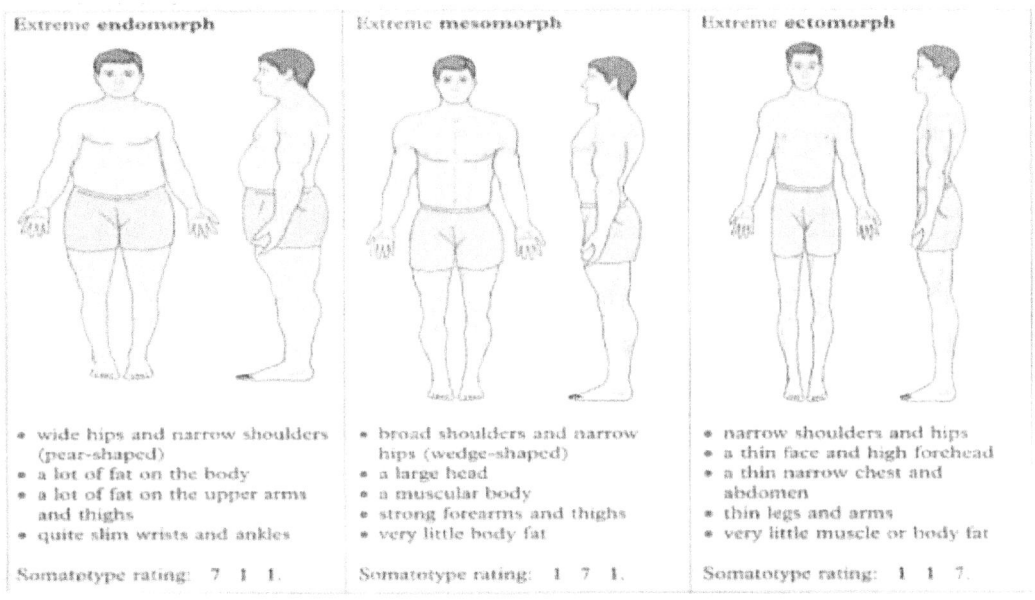

Extreme endomorph

- wide hips and narrow shoulders (pear-shaped)
- a lot of fat on the body
- a lot of fat on the upper arms and thighs
- quite slim wrists and ankles

Somatotype rating: 7 1 1.

Extreme mesomorph

- broad shoulders and narrow hips (wedge-shaped)
- a large head
- a muscular body
- strong forearms and thighs
- very little body fat

Somatotype rating: 1 7 1.

Extreme ectomorph

- narrow shoulders and hips
- a thin face and high forehead
- a thin narrow chest and abdomen
- thin legs and arms
- very little muscle or body fat

Somatotype rating: 1 1 7.

Is there any modern backing for the body/criminality debate?

Does the body shape constitute the personality type. Your thoughts?

Positivist theories of Crime

The Positivist theory

Positive approach theorists believe that criminal behaviour is the product of a complex interaction between biology and environmental or social conditions.

Positive theorists primarily focused on biological and physiological factors of criminal behaviour. This school believed that criminals are born, and not made (Nature not Nurture); this school also advocated the XYY theory (abnormal chromosomes) and physical characteristics (the size of the jaw and teeth) determined the path a criminal could take.

The late 1800 saw the dawn of the positive school of thought or theory. This school of thought saw the beginning of the view that scientific research and investigation was vital to ensure that theories have the basics and not theories based on ideas.

Positive school of thought sought to investigate the causes of crime, why it happened and what causes it. During this progressive and dynamic time interest and investigation into other sciences were growing, such as the natural sciences (physics, biology, chemistry etc.) were being developed.

Positive theorists believed that;

1.   Human behaviour is determined and not a matter of free will.
2.   Whether a person actually behaves in that way and whether that behaviour is defined as a crime depend on environmental or social conditions.
3   Criminals are fundamentally different from non-criminals.
4   Social scientists can be objective in their work.
5   Crime is frequently caused by multiple factors.
6   Biology or genetics only gives an individual a **predisposition** to behave in a certain way.

Enrico Ferri

Ferri developed the field of criminal sociology and was the forefather of the positivist school of criminology; he outright denied that free will was an aspect of criminology.

He was a positive theorist, who determined and claimed that a person's environment, the economy and society determined their criminality.

He claimed that criminality could be defined by a person's';

- Physical factors, including race, geographical location and climate
- Anthropological factors such as age, sex, biological and physical condition
- Social factors, i.e. economic conditions, religion and general customs

Ferri was the advocate of the theory of a person being a "born criminal," to designate Lombroso's atavistic type of criminal, and developed one of his basic ideas: a scientific classification of criminals.

Ferri's classification included the following:

1. The born or instinctive criminal, who carries from birth, through unfortunate heredity from his progenitors, a reduced resistance to criminal stimuli and also an evident and precocious propensity to crime

2. The insane criminal, affected by a clinically identified mental disease or by a neuro-psychopathic condition which groups him with the mentally diseased

3. The passional criminal, who, in two varieties, the criminal through passion (a prolonged and chronic mental state), or through emotion (explosive or unexpected mental state), represents a type at the opposite pole from the criminal due to congenital tendencies

4. The occasional criminal who constitutes the majority of lawbreakers and is the product of family as well as, social milieu more than of abnormal personal physio-mental conditions

5. The habitual criminal, or rather, the criminal by acquired habit, who is mostly a product of the social environment in which, due to abandonment by his family, lack of education, poverty, [and] bad companions..., already in his childhood, begins as an occasional offender.[9]

Ferri claimed that it was more important to prevent crime than to punish for it, he claimed that crime prevention was in the hands of the State, the State he claimed, could reduce crime by providing social housing and parks, equally important, the ability to marry or divorce with freedom.

Ferri classified five types of offenders;

1.   The born or instinctive criminal, who is a criminal from birth

2.   The insane criminal, those affected by mental illnesses

3.   The passional, criminal, due to either emotional or mental illness

4.   The occasional criminal, due to family background or family traits

5.   The habitual criminal, an offender who from childhood or adulthood undertakes criminal behaviour, continuing this from habit.

---

[9] T. Sellin, "Enrico Ferri," in Pioneers in Criminology, H. Mannheim, ed., 2nd ed., Montclair, NJ: Patterson Smith, 1972, pp. 378–79.

This was a very progressive theory in the 1800s. Positives did not believe in the classical theory of free will, they believed that a person's environment impacts their behaviour, for instance, if a person has no food they will starve if they do not get food, (steal or die..!), they will have no choice but to steal. Positive school of thought stated that in order to reduce crime the state needed to ensure that the reasons for the crime must be reduced or eradicated.

Franz Joseph Gall

Franz Joseph Gall (1758–1828)

Around 1800, Franz Joseph Gall, a German neuro-anatomist and physiologist who pioneered study of the human brain as the source of mental faculties, developed the practice of cranioscopy, a technique by which to infer behaviours or characteristics from external examination of the skull (cranium).

According to Gall, a person's strengths, weaknesses, morals, proclivities, character, and personality could be determined by physical characteristics of his or her skull.

The object of my researches is the brain. The cranium is only a faithful cast of the external surface of the brain, and is consequently but a minor part of the principal object. Franz Joseph Gall

Gall mapped out the location of 27 "brain organs" on the human skull. A bump or depression in a particular area of the skull would indicate a strength or weakness in that particular area. For example, several areas of Gall's map of the skull were believed to correspond to that person's tendencies to engage in criminal or deviant acts. One area corresponded to the tendency to commit murder; another area corresponded to the tendency to steal.

Although not widely accepted in Europe, the English elite used Gall's ideas to justify the oppression of individuals whose skulls had bumps or depressions in the wrong areas. The practice also was widely accepted in America between 1820 and 1850.

Franz Joseph Gall

Although crude, somewhat ridiculous by today's standards, Gall's efforts had significant impact on subsequent research that attempted to identify the brain as the origin of behaviour.

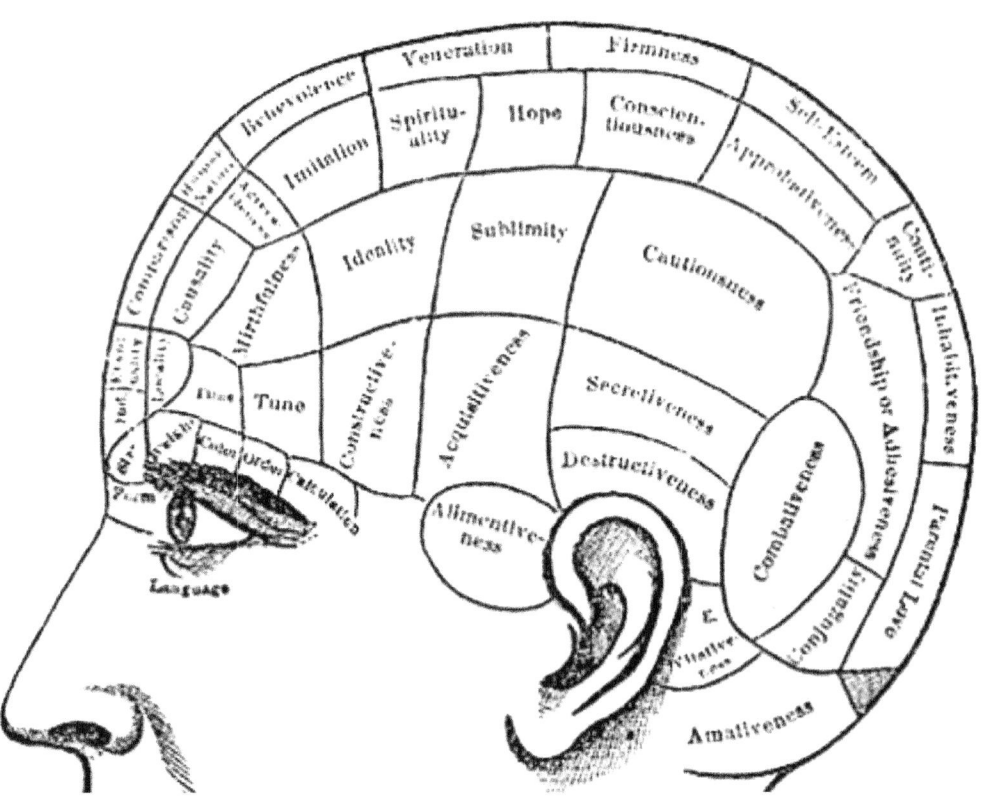

Charles Darwin

Charles Darwin (1809–1882)

Darwin described his theories in two main publications: (1) On the Origin of Species by Means of Natural Selection, or the Preservation of Favoured Races in the Struggle for Life (1859) and (2) The Descent of Man and Selection in Relation to Sex (1871).

In On the Origin of Species, Darwin detailed the theory that organisms evolve over generations through a process of natural selection. Darwin reached his conclusions which supported his observations through evidence that he collected during a sea voyage on-board the boat, the HMS Beagle, during the 1830s.

The Descent of Man and Selection in Relation to Sex applied Darwin's theory to human evolution and described the theory of sexual selection. Although he had earlier hinted that natural selection and evolution could and should be applied to the development of man, others (Thomas Huxley in 1863, Alfred Wallace in 1864) had actually applied his theories to the human animal first.

The publication of Charles Darwin's theory of evolution in "On the Origin of Species" in 1859 was the stepping stone which theorists such as Cesare Lombroso used in the formation of their theories of criminal behaviour. His views on the "born criminal" suggested that offenders were less evolved than non- criminals. His research established that it was possible to identify a criminal through their atavistic or apelike appearances or behaviours. The atavistic explanation has been disproven however, it established the process of scientific inquiry that characterised the positive school of criminology.

Charles Darwin

Not a theorist of criminology, however I would just like to mention this progressive naturist and geologist, his theories that an animal's development dependent on their environment, but also, how the adaption or destruction of that environment impacted their behaviour.

Do you believe that the environmental factor is important in crime and criminality?

John Locke

John Locke (1632–1704)

Locke was more interested in an individual and their inalienable absolute rights than the social contract put forward by Hobbes, both philosophers worked in similar time frames and although Locke agreed with some of Hobbes theories he believed that surrendering the right to self-govern in favour of the protection of sovereignty rules came with a social contract with provisions such as reciprocity.

'To understand political power aright, and derive it from its original, we must consider what state all men are naturally in, and that is a state of perfect freedom to order their actions and dispose of their possessions and persons as they think fit... A state also of equality, wherein all the power and jurisdiction is reciprocal, no one having more than another; there being nothing more evident than that creatures of the same species and rank... the use of the same faculties, should also be equal one amongst another without subordination or subjection...'

Locke was an advent of power where power is necessary, or that there should only be as much power as was needed for the good of society. He stated that power should be given to the people who are elected by the people for the good of the people however, not those whose power derives from hereditary powers or favour. *'And all this to be directed to no other end but the peace, safety, and public good of the people'* Locke spoke of the 'social contract' with such knowledge and rigour it would have given the impression that this social contract was an actual event in history for which he has studied and become proficient and knowledgeable'.

His book was at the forefront of the Rule of Law, whereby fair procedure and the presumption of innocence. Beccaria believed that laws could not be just and fair if the general public were not aware of them also, the restrictions and sanctions clearly defined, that the law should not be retrospective (*guilty today for something you did yesterday, which was legal at the time you did it*) also, that the judiciary should not have the scope to interpret legislation unless in set rules. Furthermore, he believed that punishment should be a deterrent to the general public, not just the individual involved and also that morals have no place in sentencing for legal breaches.

Rule of law. *'It is better for the law to rule than one of its citizens'* ~Aristotle (however it is vital that that ruling law to be ruled lawfully also)

The Rule of Law

1. No sanction without breach

2. No one is above the law and all must be subject to jurisdiction in the same courts

3. Common law system with judge-made law secures the rights of individuals State must use its power according to agreed rules and not arbitrarily.

Article 40.1 of the Irish Constitution states:

All citizens shall, as human persons, be held equal before the law. This shall not be held to mean that the State shall not in its enactments have due regard to differences of capacity, physical and moral, and of social function.

The rule of law, was popularised by AV Dicey in 1885, the Rule of law implies absolute supremacy of law. It guarantees that an individual can ascertain with reasonable certainty what legal powers are available to the government if an individual's rights are infringed, as stated in

Article 40.1 of the Irish Constitution states:

All citizens shall, as human persons, be held equal before the law. This shall not be held to mean that the State shall not in its enactments have due regard to differences of capacity, physical and moral, and of social function. The contrast between the rule of men and the rule of law is first found in Plato's Statesman and Laws and Aristotle's Politics, where the rule of law implies both obedience to positive law and formal checks and balances on rulers and judiciary.

It does not exempt the officials or others from the duty of obedience to the law which governs other citizens or from jurisdiction of ordinary tribunals. However, this is now subject to the Supremacy of EU law.

For my part two core meanings of the rule of law are essential to an understanding of our public law…The rule of law is a term of political philosophy or institutional morality. It conveys the idea of government not under men but under laws….In its second sense…its general focus is to constrain the abuse of official power. It protects a citizen's right to legal certainty in respect of interference with his liberties. It guarantees access to justice. It ensures procedural fairness over much of the range of administrative decision-making by officials. ~ Lord Steyn.

Jean-Jacques Rousseau (1712–1778)

Unlike Locke, Rousseau believed in the theory of the "social contract" however, he further defined this as more in terms of 'social order' than the 'social contract'. Rousseau believed that man is inherently good. 'Man is born innocent and good, free and equal, but the corrupting powers of civilisation are responsible for the evil situation in which he finds himself'.

This belief in the inherent good of man was defined further when Rousseau stated that the inherent goodness of man was corrupted by the past and past events. However, he believed that this still held man in chains due to being held to a higher order in the social contract. He also believed that the people reigned supreme and no sovereign can remove that right, he also believed that society thrives when the masses are happy, *'and in which each, while uniting himself with all, may still obey himself alone, and remain as free as before'.*[10]

The theory Rousseau put forward was that the general population as well as the individual are under the power of the "general will". He stated that people will obey when forced to obey, he stated that society did well under this pretence, however, he believed that societies thrived when the force to obey was less prevalent; however this theory has been debunked by modern philosophers.

Rousseau recognises that self-preservation is only one principle of motivation for the actions of humans or what differentials humans

---

[10] LOCKE AND ROUSSEAU:. Jamie Gianoutsos.
http://www.baylor.edu/content/services/document.php?id=37670

from animals the difference, he stated, was the human souls' and, the ability to empathise and, feel guilt or pity.

This is *"an innate repugnance to see his fellow suffer"*. Another difference between humans and animals, is that humans are *"if acting legally and within the laws of the land"* free agents to come and go as they please and have the ability to reason any situation which they may find themselves part of.

The Social Contract

Chapter three – Modern theories and theorists

11

Modern Theories of Crime

Modern criminology has taken the works of its predecessors, and built on them, the development of modern criminology can be attributed to theorists such as Durkheim, Sutherland and Merton's.

---

11 http://study.com/cimages/videopreview/the-rational-choice-theory-of-criminology_137098.jpg

Anomie or Strain Theory

This school believes that people commit crimes when they see no legitimate way to achieve their goals. This theory may explain why there is more crime among the economically disadvantaged. Anomie or Strain theorists believed that crime was as a direct result of lower class frustration and anger. According to strain theory, people feel the strain when they are exposed to cultural goals that they are unable to obtain because they do not have access to culturally approved means of achieving those goals

Robert Merton in 1938 wrote about a major contradiction in the U.S. between cultural goals and social structure. He called the contradiction anomie. For Merton, the contradiction between the cultural goal of achieving wealth and the social structure's inability to provide legitimate institutional means for achieving the goal (Merton. P, 1938)[12]

Society defines success in terms of certain goals, but does not always provide the means or opportunity for people to reach these goals. Merton argued that the limited availability of legitimate institutionalised means to wealth puts a strain on people.

People adapt through:

- Conformity—playing the game, achieve goals by legitimate means
- Innovation—pursuing wealth by illegitimate means and finding ways to achieve.
- Ritualism— not actively pursuing wealth but dreaming about it.
- Retreatism—dropping out, not even trying.
- Rebellion—rejecting the goal of wealth, and the institutional means of getting it and creating a new system.

---

[12] Merton. P, 1938; "Science, Technology and Society in Seventeenth Century England", Osiris, Vol. IV, pt. 2, pp. 360–632. Bruges: St. Catherine Press, 1938

Merton also argued that individuals' perceptions of economic and social inequality lead to feelings of envy, mistrust, and aggression, this leads to the lower classes feeling both deprived and embittered, and some turn to crime to reduce the feelings of inequality.

Social Learning Theory

Edwin H. Sutherland (in his theory of differential association) was the first 20th-century criminologist to argue that criminal behaviour was learned. This theory, modified, remains one of the most influential theories of crime causation. Sutherland's theory that persons' who become criminals do so because of contacts with criminal patterns and, isolation from anti-criminal patterns.

Warr and Stafford (1991:862) studied the mechanism by which delinquency is socially transmitted. They compared the effect of peer attitudes and effects of peer behaviour and found that delinquency stemmed rather from behaviour of peers than the consequence of attitudes acquired from peers.

This means that Sutherland's assertion that attitude of peers is the major factor of delinquency is incomplete. The attitudes of adolescents indeed do influence delinquency. "However, quite apart from the attitudes of adolescents and those of their friends, the behaviour of friends has a strong, independent effect on adolescents' behaviour.[13]

Social Learning Theorists believe that:

1. Criminal behaviour is learned (it is not invented): In interactions with others in intimate groups
2. Differential associations vary: Intensity, priority, duration, frequency
3. Learning includes (a) techniques; (b) attitudes that are contained in "definitions" of the legal code

---

[13] Mark Warr, Mark Stafford(1991). The influence of delinquent peers: What they think or what they do?. Criminology.

4. Delinquency is caused by an excess of definitions in favour of law violation
5. Learning criminal behaviour involves the same processes and mechanisms as other behaviours

Social Control Theory

Social control depends on people's anticipating the consequences of their behaviour; people who believe they have little to lose are more likely to become deviant

Sutherland's theory, that persons who become criminal do so because of contacts with criminal patterns, and isolation from anti-criminal patterns. Individuals tightly bonded to conventional social groups less likely to be delinquent

1. Family

2. School

3. Non-delinquent peers

There are four elements of the social bond

1. Attachment: affection for and sensitivity to others

2. Commitment: to conventional society

3. Involvement: in conventional activities

4. Belief: in obeying conventional rules

The most detailed elaboration of modern social control theory is attributed to Travis Hirsch, who wrote the 1969 book, Causes of Delinquency.[14] (Hirschi.T, 1969). Hirsch argued that delinquency should be expected if a juvenile is not properly socialised by establishing a strong bond to society, consisting of:

- Attachment to others, strong social attachments encourages conformity and lesson criminal behaviours.
- Opportunity, the greater a person's access to legitimate opportunity, the greater the advantages of conformity
- Involvement in conventional activities, extensive involvement in legitimate activities inhibits deviance.
- Belief in the moral order and law, strong belief in conventional morality and respect for authority figures restrain tendencies toward deviance.

---

[14] Travis Hirschi 1969; University of California Press,

Labelling Theory

Labelling Theory

Labelling theory suggests that people defined themselves as society sees them, labelling can start in childhood, the labels can go from they're a good kid, just a bit wild, and progress to they're a bad apple, they are. Therefore, crime is not always defined by the behaviour of criminals, but to society's reaction to it. (Reread my own statement in the beginning, of socially acceptable criminal behaviours)

Labelling can go from the community to the criminal justice system, criminals rarely see themselves as criminals, they often state things like, they had it coming, r they have insurance.

The labelling theory argues that once a person commits a first criminal act and gets processed in the system, they are labelled negatively as a criminal.

The label becomes a self-fulfilling prophecy

Labelling theory suggests that people in power decide what acts are crimes, and the act of labelling someone a criminal is what makes him a criminal. Once a person is labelled a criminal, society takes away his opportunities, which may ultimately lead to more criminal behaviour.

Once a criminal is convicted or incarcerated it is difficult to remove that label, society labels them and getting a job can prove difficult, leading them straight back into crime due to necessity or vengeance.

If you refer back to race and ethnicity you can see for example, young travellers being labelled as "trouble" etc., this label, then defines all travellers' behaviour as deviant, this furthers the social isolation and labelling and creating a vicious circle, if I am trouble then I'll be trouble and so it goes on.

Radical Theory

Radical theories argue that capitalism requires people to compete against each other in the pursuit of material wealth.

The more unevenly wealth is distributed; the more likely people are to find persons weaker than themselves that they can take advantage of in their pursuit of wealth. These theories of crime causation are generally based on a Marxist theory, of class struggle.

Radical Theorists believe that;

1. Society is seen to "function" in terms of the general interests of a ruling class rather than "everyone".
2. The potential for class conflict is always present - a ruling class has to continually act to reproduce its domination of other classes in society.

For instance, there is a belief amongst some racial theory camp that class structure produces social control, such instances can be explained, for instance, social welfare, this is a payment to those who cannot afford the cost of living and who are either unemployed or disabled etc., radical theorists claim this is a form of social control, keeping the lower classes poor with institutionalism and over reliance on the ruling classes for their means, the ruling class in return abusing this by making rules that benefit the ruling classes while dressing it up to appear like "they are being supported and helped"

Some theorists of criminology believe that only when capitalism is replaced by socialism, will there be a solution to the crime problem.

Deterrence Theory

This theory advocates that an individual chooses to commit a crime, but this choice is influence by the fear of punishment. Unlike choice theory which states that a person will weigh up the choices before deciding on the criminal behaviour, deterrence on the other hand emphasises that people will not commit a crime if the punishment outweigh the pleasure, or that

"it's just not worth it", in essence stopping the criminal act before its even taken place by ensuring that any offenders are aware of the punishment and any sanctions which will be imposed.

This punishment must be severe enough to prevent the offender from partaking in it in the first place. (This sounds familiar, Neo-classical..!) However, some offenders are still of the thought that should they get caught some police officers will not pursue a conviction due to the relatively minor offence. In order for punishment to be deterrence, then justice must not only be done, it must be seen to be done. However, research has shown that simply increasing police presence or extending sentences for offences has not brought crime down.

Assumptions of the Deterrence Theory

Hedonistic Calculus - Humans are rational, thoughtful, people, and consider the consequences of their actions. The theory that society has a fear of formal punishment is the key restraint for crime - Banking on police and prisons as primary concern of a potential criminal.

Can the Deterrence Theory operate at macro level or micro level? Explain.

- Macro = compare cities, states, countries
- Micro = individuals

Specific deterrence – focuses on the offender

- Seeks to prevent a particular offender from engaging in repeat criminality

General deterrence – works by example

- Seeks to prevent others from committing crimes similar to the one for which a particular offender is being sentenced.

An Economic Model of Crime

An economic model of crime claims that a person will make the same decision when faced with the same consequences, for instance if the reward is the same as the last offence then they will commit again, if they find and easy target they will strike again, this is why some offenders will return to burgle the same house a number of times, this could be due to the fact that the house is easy to access with an easy target and easy goods to sell, and also may be down to the fact that the victim may replace the stolen items quickly with more good quality and easy to offload goods making it attractive, if they can commit a crime knowing the rewards and costs in advance they will probably follow the same course of action.

Deterrence and Econometrics

The justice model stresses or the just deserts model advocates that, if an offender breaks the law they should get punished. Utilitarian punishment philosophy is based on the theory that punishment is a necessary evil. It is both protection and deterrence.

The economic model of crime stresses that criminal behaviour follows a calculation whereby the criminal explores the perceived costs, rewards, and risks of alternative actions.

Deterrence aims to ensure that victims are not soft targets, and that the general public should ensure that rewards of crime are reduced by;

- Concealing goods
- Removing goods from public sight
- Identifying property with markings

Environmentalism

Also associated with

- Rational choice theory
- Routine activity theory

Theorists claim that offenders are more likely to offend in an area they know well, this increases their chances of escape and evade capture.

Research suggests that burglars will commit crimes in areas they know well and times they know that there is less likelihood of getting caught, this means that some areas were high target areas with high instances of burglary in specific areas.

Routine Activity Theory

Routine activities theory holds that lifestyles contribute to the volume and type of crime found in society. This new perspective within the modern schools of criminological believed that the contributions of routine activities theory and situational crime prevention, as well as the ecological approaches contribute to criminal behaviour or lack of it. Crime is likely to occur when a motivated offender and a suitable target come together in absence of a capable guardian.

Routine activities theory extends the classical approach. It however does go deeper in definition, Routine activities theory claims that criminals balance the pros and cons long before they commit the crime and only commit it when they have weighed all sides.

Routine activities theorists claim that:

- self-interest motivates criminal offenders to commit criminal acts;
- Many individuals may be motivated to break laws.

The better the reward the more pleasure is derived from it, such as car theft and joyriding; these crimes give positive rewards for negative behaviour and may induce a person to commit a crime.

Protection does lesson crimes, CCTV, gates, security guards, this is due to the fact that the cost to the offender is higher in terms of time and effort and lessening the attractiveness of the target or victim.

(Example; Crime is likely to occur when a motivated offender and a suitable target come together in absence of a capable guardian.)

Rational Choice

Rational choice theory holds that criminality is the result of conscious choice. –Individuals commit crime when the benefits outweigh the risks.

Rational choice theory focuses on the situational aspects of criminal behaviour and stresses that a criminal rationally chooses both the crime to commit and the target of the crime. Rational choice can be explained as an event that occurs when an offender decides to risk breaking the law after considering his or her own need for money, personal values or learning experiences and how well a target is protected, how affluent the neighbourhood is or how efficient the local police are. Rational choice theorists are concerned with the conditions which promote crime and enhance criminality within society. It is also about reducing crime by reducing the opportunities to commit crime.

N.B there are numerous perceptions of behaviour from the point of view of the criminal, I will deal with three. Perceptions of crime from a criminal's point of view, criminals when questioned about their criminal behaviour tend to state some of the following as their interpretation at the time of the commission of the offence, they tended to;

- overestimate the money they receive from crime,
- they is no choice, legitimate work is not available,
- They are overly optimistic about getting away with their crimes.

(Example: This theory is also known as the situational theory; this explains that each person uses choice in deciding whether or not to commit a crime. i.e. they weigh the proceeds of the criminal act against their perceived punishment "if" they get caught.)

Ethnicity and Crime

Each individual Country has specific ethnic groups which are far more likely involved with the criminal justice system than others. The ethnic groups which have this elevated status can vary from Country to Country and Continent to Continent. Ireland does not have much empirical or statistics results on other ethnicities as of yet as research in this area is not commonplace, however, there is some research regarding travellers, their race is white Irish, their ethnicity is traveller, (although not defined by the state as ethnic) but defined by Sinead Ni Shuinear (1994, 2002) argues, after Barth, that Travellers are definitely an ethnic group:

- They are biologically self-reproducing (Travellers marry Travellers, you cannot become a Traveller)[15]
- They share fundamental cultural values. They make up a boundaried social group in terms of communication (their own language, Cant or Gammon
- They identify themselves (as Travellers)

Therefore some attention will be paid to this ethnic group before taking International statistics into consideration. Firstly, Traveller men are between five and 11 times more likely than other men to be imprisoned, while Traveller women face a risk of imprisonment as much as 18 to 22 times higher than that of the general population.

It is clear that in proportion to male travellers, female travels are at a higher risk of being sentenced to a prison sentence. The majority of sentenced being meted to travellers is for theft and property offences. Travellers are 11 times more likely to be stopped and questioned by the Gardaí than a settled person and the unemployment rate for travellers aged 15-24 is over 70%.[16]

---

[15] This definition is not as yet been accepted by the establishment
[16] The Irish Penal Reform Trust. Travellers in the Irish Prison System

Ethnicity and Crime

In the UK suggests that black people whose families originate from the Caribbean in the 1940s are more likely to be criminalised, also figures from recent statistics in the UK state that Asians are 11 times more likely to be stopped and questioned at the borders, while Asians were twice as likely to be stopped and searched as white counterparts. While black people are 6 times more likely to be stopped and searched than their white counterparts, and 6 times more likely to be arrested than white people.

The varying reasons for the higher numbers of black, Asian and travellers being arrested, charged or jailed for offences may be explained by the fact that these ethnic groups high a higher proportion of younger males and females than the white population and crime peaks between ages of 21 and 24 meaning there are simply more younger people in these ethnic groups than white accounting for the higher rates. (This is debatable, just has statistical backing). (Povis and Walmsley (2002)).

There appears to be a variety of factors which are responsible for the variations and higher crime and sentencing rates. Travellers have a much lower school finishing rate than settled people and some Asian and black groups have this low levels of education which can place them at a higher risk of offending means that they are less able to achieve their goals through legitimate means, and are likely to experience one or more factors that put them at risk of offending.' However this explanation places the emphasis on the ethnicity and not the individual offender. This may even suggest that offenders are victims of institutionalised racism.[17]

---

[17] Hiro, Dilip. Black British, White British: A History of Race Relations in Britain. London:Paladin, 1992
A press release from the Home Office Press (11 July 2006) entitled 'Criminal Justice System tackling Racism and Racist Crime'

Feminist Theory

Feminist criminology emphasises gender issues and seeks to develop an appreciation of the role of women in the causes of crime, victimisation of women in the criminal justice system, and the control of crime.

Feminists see women and girls are doubly affected by theories and crime, Feminist theories of crime ask questions such as

- Do traditional male-centred theories of crime apply to women?"
- What explains the universal fact that women are far less likely than men to involve themselves in criminal activity?

It wasn't until the 1970 that this school of criminology was born, this was due to the perceived rise in criminality by women, the feminist theory of criminality worked on the premise that female committed crimes for different reasons than men, it was also a feminist theory that the criminal justice system was patriarchal and crime was defined by men for men and women were not catered for either in criminality or punishment.

Lombroso (p. 27) believed that women who committed crimes were doubly deviant; they even went so far as to describe female criminals as looking physically like men and normal women were not criminally inclined. In the 1970s, Dr Klein set out to debunk these theories and determined that female criminality was in part due to economic needs rather than deviancy. In Ireland in 2015 only 3.5% of the prison population were female; this insight shows the levels of female offenders showing the gender gap interred.

Types of feminism

- Liberal Feminism: Gender differences in crime rates traced to gender differences in socialisation
- Marxist Feminism: Women forced to commit crime to survive in capitalist society
- Radical Feminism: Patriarchy precedes capitalism; gender more important than class
- Socialist Feminism: Sees capitalism and patriarchy as equally important
- Multicultural Feminism: Stresses importance of race and ethnicity along with gender and class.[18]

Feminist theories of crime suggest that traditional theories of crime do not apply to females, to date, there is little empirical evidence or data specifically for female criminality, however, the limited research does show that the geographical, social and economic backgrounds of female offenders are similar to their male counterparts. Feminist criminology focuses on trying to recognise female offending from the feminist point of view, which believes that women are faced with special circumstances living in a patriarchal society.

Modern feminist theories of criminology

Research in the 1990s has divided opinion with its theories lying with social theories of crime, that women commit crimes because of social needs, and not because of any natural predisposition. Research in this area is still on-going with emphasis on gender bias and disparity in sentencing rather than female criminalities causes.

Criminology's gender blindness

"Our knowledge is still in its infancy. In comparison with the massive documentation on all aspects of male delinquency and criminality, the amount of work carried out on the area of women and crime is

---

[18] Steve E. Barkan. 2015. Criminology: A Sociological Understanding, Prentice Hall

extremely limited".   Carol Smart (1977) Women, Crime and Criminology

The theories as to why there are less female offenders than male;

1. Biological: women are naturally less criminal than men (Lombroso)
2. Masked Crime: women's routine activities allow them greater opportunities for concealing crime (Pollak)
3. Control: girls and young women are subject to more control than boys and young men
4. Gender and Strain: women's maternal roles lessen the impact of economic status deprivation
5. Chivalry: Police/Gardaí and Courts deal with women more leniently: evidence patchy

Age and Crime

Age has long been a major factor in criminal behaviour, as is the notion that criminality reduces with age. Criminal age peaks in the mid-20s, with the highest instances of criminal behaviour in youths age 18 to 24. The explanations for the peak stem from age, stamina, agility, speed to aggression. Teenagers have few connections to traditional adult institutions, such as work and family. [19]

Teens are tempted by the quick money and rewards such as power or status and the pleasure seeking adrenaline and sensual pleasures. Teens and young adults have no responsibility and are supported by their careers, and have no reasoning as to the consequences of their actions, especially financial consequences, "if they commit crime, they will not be expected to pay their fines, their parents are expected to".

Age/Crime Curve

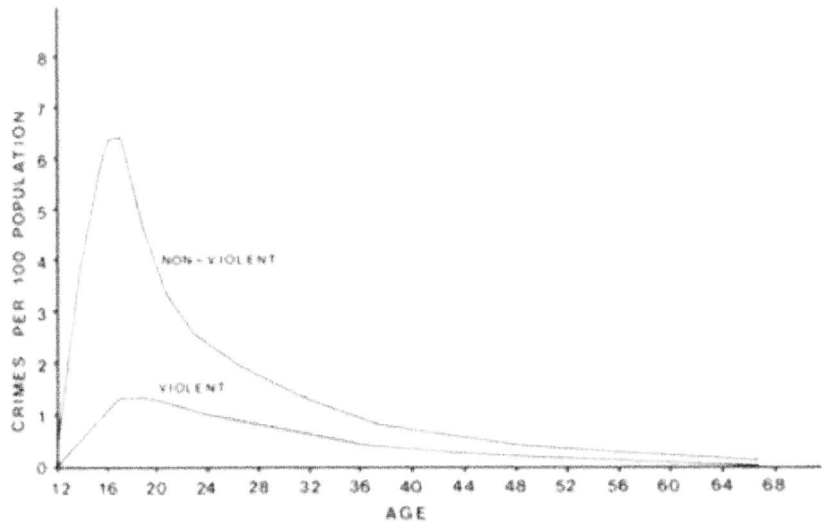

Deviance in teenage years is often defined or described as the teen "just growing up". As teen's progress into adulthood after the peak

---

[19] Warr, Mark. (1998) "Life-Course Transitions and Desistance from Crime." Criminology

age of 24 changes are prominent in their lives,[20] this is when many "grow up", there have been 6 changes identified as important in the decline in criminal behaviour after the peak age and adulthood assumed from 25 years on. [21]

Distribution of Crime. American Journal of Sociology

1. People have better access to legitimate sources of material goods and excitement: jobs, home, alcohol and sex.

2. People are "expected to grow up" and increase their responsibility, deviance is no longer acceptable and maturity is expected from society around them.

3. People don't "hang out" with their friends as much when they get older, friendship is replaced with relationships and assumed responsibility

4. Legally and socially responsible for deviant behaviour.

5. As people get older the types of crimes may also change, fraud and gambling increase due to the fact that they is an assumption that there is less risk and more return in these crimes.

---

[20] Jolin, Annette, and Gibbons, Don. (1987) "Age Patterns in Criminal Involvement." International Journal of Offender Therapy and Comparative Criminology

[21] Steffensmeier, Darrell; Allan, Emilie; Harer, MILES; and Streifel, Cathy. (1989)"Age and the

6. As a person gets older they analyse and become more aware of their actions and the consequences, this leads to a decline in the self and self wants. The meaning of life is questioned more and how their actions affect others.

The trends seem to increase in urban and populated areas; this is in part due to access to the items of their desire. Peer pressure is another cause, other friends daring and betting they won't commit crimes, or gang affiliation or "belonging" requires deviance and criminal activity as a prerequisite to joining.

Until the peak at 25 there is very little in the crime rates and deviancy in females and males (excluding prostitution which a dominantly female profession).

The most common finding across countries, groups, and historical eras is that crime tends to be a young persons' game.

Mental Disorder and Crime

Section 3 of the Mental Health Act, states, mental illness, severe dementia or significant intellectual disability where—

(a)   because of the illness, disability or dementia, there is a serious likelihood of the person concerned causing immediate and serious harm to himself or herself or to other persons, or

(b)   (i) because of the severity of the illness, disability or dementia, the judgment of the person concerned is so impaired that failure to admit the person to an approved centre would be likely to lead to a serious deterioration in his or her condition or would prevent the administration of appropriate treatment that could be given only by such admission, and

(ii) The reception, detention and treatment of the person concerned in an approved centre would be likely to benefit or alleviate the condition of that person to a material extent.

The medical definition of mental illness is different, it is defined as *"a mental disorder is considered to be a group of clinically significant behaviours or patterns that cannot be an expectable response to a particular event or situation and must be considered a manifestation of a behavioural, psychological, or biological dysfunction in the person"*.

Police and Gardaí are poorly equipped to deal with offenders with mental health issues and this can result in unintentional abuse of positions, and also necessary treatment or sentencing are not being identified and recognised. There are calls for more training in real life situations for the Police/Gardaí, this is essential for empathy, understanding and experience. Mental illness can result in heartbreak when crime results and there is not enough training, such as the Abbeylara shooting in which a member of the Gardaí shot and killed a mentally ill man, this resulted in much more training for Gardaí in recognising and responding to mentally ill criminal behaviour.

Dealing with mental illness is now more hands on, doctors, family and trained medical staff can deal with a mentally ill offender, and those at risk of offending. The types of offences which people with mental illness tend to partake in and come before the courts are but not limited to; criminal damage, burglary, public order offences handling stolen goods shoplifting, fraud, and dishonestly. [22] The instances of abuse and public order offences rise when the mental illness is coupled with substance abuse.

Many offenders with mental illness feel that the criminal justice system punishes them for being themselves, and having an illness which is "them". Many offenders with mental illnesses are involuntarily committed and given treatment, there are of course those who agree to being committed and treated, but where the offender refuses then commitment at the central mental hospital may be ordered. This in part is society's need that justice needs to be seen to be done. It is vital going forward that possible offenders who have mental illnesses need to be identified much faster than they already are, to recognise the offences before they are committed because of the behaviours of the mentally ill person.

Mentally ill offenders can be treated in specialised hospitals or in prisons, depending on the severity of the mental illness and the tools available in prisons. Unfortunately, there are still mentally ill offenders who are not diagnosed, at all, either prior to their incarceration, or during their stay, leaving them unprepared for the release and destined to repeat their offending. Raising awareness of mental illness is vital for all those in and outside of the criminal justice system, removing the stigma of mental illness so those affected by mental illness are more likely to come forward to seek treatment.

---

[22] (Bean, 2009).

John Rawls

John Bordley Rawls (1921 – 2002)

Rawls' theory is based upon three elements: a vision of society as it ought to be; a view of moral theory and its significance; and the derivation of principles which will enable an expression of that vision to be enunciated so as to reflect moral theory. (Curzon, 1995)

Rawl attempted to define social justice in the context of a social contract; he uses the theory of the original position to define the ideal social order.

The perception of justice for Rawls starts with "justice as fairness". This is based on the original moral theory of utilitarianism (although I am not convinced of this being utilitarian, but Rawlsonian "his own moral theory").

The Original position

The hypothetical society which was chosen under Rawls "original position" revolved around a congress that objectivity discussed and decided in a set of fundamental principles which were at the forefront of their society. This society would be governed on the principles of what are objectively "just" (not one individual persons interpretation of just but that of the whole society)

This theory is based on the presumption that people and society's consent to being governed. He claimed that: "the basic structure of society, or more exactly, the way in which the major social institutions distribute fundamental rights and duties and determine the division of advantages from social cooperation. By major institutions I understand the political constitution and the principal economic and social arrangements".

Rawl committed a lot of his research to the theories of social organisation, the social organisation theory would suggest that people are not free to choose or to make rational choices or make just decisions and inherently civil disobedience will result in punishments. This society will only exist where there is fair treatment of every individual.

Rawl however, led this theory from a utopian point of view, whereby everyone will do well if they are taken care of within society, the good of the greater over the good of the few...he stated that: "everyone is presumed to act justly and to do his part in upholding just institutions". (Surely then this means that Rawls new society would have to be subjected to compliance?).

The veil of ignorance

In order for fairness and impartiality in society, it is according to Rawls, imperative that all bias is removed. For instance, all bias towards the rich or poor and religious or non-religious, advantaged or disadvantaged need to be removed before we can see impartial procedures. The principle of the veil of ignorance is significant insofar as it removed any personal perception of what good is it is the good of society as a general rule than any individual.

This principle of the veil of ignorance ensures consistency and fairness in the division of wealth, food, social and religion;[23] therefore the theories of the social contract emerge. The Social contract consists of:

• The original position with representatives

---

[23] my own interpretation

- The two principles of justice structured by the basic principle of fair and just

- The actual society with no bias towards any persons with 'fairness is justice' at its core.

The representatives of this new social order must be in the original position; this is to ensure that there is a free, just and fair social order. The original order is based on each and every person and representative not knowing their social order when determining the rules of fair and just, for instance, the persons or representatives would not know if they were a lowly servant or royalty, they would have no idea of social standing or financial status or their religious affiliation when they are defining this new social structure. [24]

The Veil of Ignorance

The representatives do not know anything about the persons they represent: their sex, race, physical handicaps, social class, or conception of the good. It is important that the representatives are aware of psychology and sociology, for instance, that humans remember the past, anticipate the future, and also socialises and interacts in the present, they are of all abilities and take part in all types of social interactions, and finally they know that there are those in this original position who are sick or disabled

Two principles of justice

These two types of the principles of justice:

- Political justice: rights of the many outweigh the rights of the few.
- Social justice: each person is to have an equal right to basic liberties and social and economic inequalities are in the

---

[24] John Rawls. A THEORY OF JUSTICE.
http://www2.econ.iastate.edu/classes/econ362/hallam/readings/rawl_justice.pdf

favour of the least advantaged and that all representative positions which are available will be available to all within society regardless of their financial, religious or social standing. [25]This principle also explains that any inequalities should be in everyone's benefit.

Rawls' theory requests the representatives to conceive of society "as a fair system of cooperation over time, from one generation to the next" and also "a structure of basic institutions we enter only by birth and exit only by death".[26]

The theoretical society will then see its citizens free and equal; these citizens will have "a capacity for a sense of justice and for a conception of the good." Which will result in "fully cooperating members of society," [27] "...to act in relation to others on terms that they also publicly endorse".

Rawls rejects Utilitarianism in the original position and the veil of ignorance due to the inability to give individual rights and freedoms and that this principle works against the original position, he further states that utility blurs the lines between individual and society misleadingly "conflat[es] all persons into one," revealing that "Utilitarianism does not take seriously the distinction between persons" also defines "Utilitarianism as the principle of utility. (What's best for the well-being of society)? It holds for all kinds of subjects ranging from the conduct of individuals to the organisation of society as a whole as well as to the law of peoples."[28]

Rawls Reasonable Citizens

Rawl refers to the reasonable citizens.

Reasonable citizens:

---

[25] John Rawls, A Theory of Justice, page 302
[26] John Rawls, A Theory of Justice. Cambridge, Mass., 1971, page 152.

[28] John Rawls, Political Liberalism, New York, NY: Columbia University Press, 1993. Page 13

"are ready to propose principles and standards as fair terms of cooperation, these citizens then abide by them willingly, given the assurance that others will likewise do so25. Likewise, "requires that when those terms are proposed as the most reasonable terms of fair cooperation, those proposing them must... think it at least reasonable for others to accept them, as free and equal citizens, and not as dominated or manipulated... under the pressure of an inferior political or social position."[29]

Rawls also recognise in the reasonable citizen those "willing to bear the consequences of the burdens of judgment.[30]" in this explanation Rawls recognises that people can and do disagree on subjects and topics, this however does not have to become a biased interpretation of the other person's judgement. Rawls defined the following such sources of disagreement or burdens of judgment as:

- Different types of evidence,
- How different people see different situations
- Principles and rules not being defined clearly,
- The diversity of human beings and their interpretation of ideals
- Two different parties have completely opposite definition of the same principle
- Some institution requiring citizens to choose one belief over another

Going back to the original position, the representatives of the ideal society under which Rawls theory of the veil of ignorance falls are given the task of selecting principles of justice that will govern the basic structure of society.

To show briefly how they will reason, let us consider whether they would choose a principle of equal opportunity, say, a principle that would make economic discrimination on the basis of race, gender, or religion unjust.

---

[29] Rawls, J. 1993In The Law of Peoples (1999) page 49
[30] Rawls, J. 1993In The Law of Peoples (1999) page 58

One of the ways in which the representatives can achieve this original position within the veil of ignorance is to remove any kids of discrimination, such as race, religion, gender or colour. Ruling out discrimination will ensure that all citizens, regardless of their race, religion, gender or colour will be afforded equal opportunities.

However, Rawls was aware that some person within society must be given more resources, power and income than other to balance the books, to pay bills or manage workers; Rawls suggest that this power can be allowed under the strictest conditions are met, such as:

(a)   the project will make life better off for the people who are now worst off, for example, by raising the living standards of everyone in the community and empowering the least advantaged persons to the extent consistent with their well-being,

(b)   access to the privileged positions is not blocked by discrimination according to irrelevant criteria.

Rawls principle of Justice

Rawls defined "justice as fairness". These principles stem from the following principles:

- Each individual is entitled equal basic liberties, freedom and liberty, the same liberty and freedom enjoyed by everyone else.
- If there are social inequalities within the citizens then then inequalities should be addressed insofar as all opportunities are available to everyone regardless of their social background. And those are least privileged get more chances than those who are privileged.
- Rawls definition, of the "fully adequate scheme of equal basic liberties." These basic liberties included:
- freedom of thought.
- liberty of conscience "liberty as applied to religious, philosophical, and moral view of our relation to the world."

- political liberties "freedom of speech and the press, and freedom of assembly"
- the freedom of association.
- freedoms specified by the liberty and integrity of the person "freedom from slavery and serfdom and freedom of movement and choice regarding occupation"
- the rights and liberties covered by the rule of law.

Rawls requires the representative in the original position to ensure basic equal liberties for all citizens. It was down to them to make a "rationally prudential choice", regarding their social contract, ensuring that all social and economic positions are to everyone's advantage, and open to all. These representatives were to use reasoning and the veil of ignorance (not knowing their special position within this new society) when deciding on a stable and democratic society. This new concept ensures basic personal liberties and freedoms "when it includes conceptions of what is of value in human life, as well as ideals of personal.

Thoughts: Sounds good on paper, but, what about inequalities in the 2nd generation, we as parents want what's best for our children, surely we would think unfair in generation 3 or 4 when some people's positions would allow them greater money, freedoms and choices than us.

The Chicago School and the US theories

The Chicago school claims that society, in the form of the community, wields a major influence on human behaviour.

It must be noted that criminological and theories of criminal behaviours developed differently in Europe and the USA. This school of thought started with "Criminality and Economic Conditions". Bonger's (1916)

In the 1900s the USA saw the growth from a rural farming landscape to an industrial city or urban landscape which was seen in 1700/1800s Britain and Europe, with it came poverty and crime similar to that seen in Europe, causes such as low pay, horrific working conditions coupled with slum housing and poor conditions gave birth to crime and poverty, the USA did not deal with the woes of city living like Europe as they had come to this growth over 100 years later so the Chicago school was born to deal with a

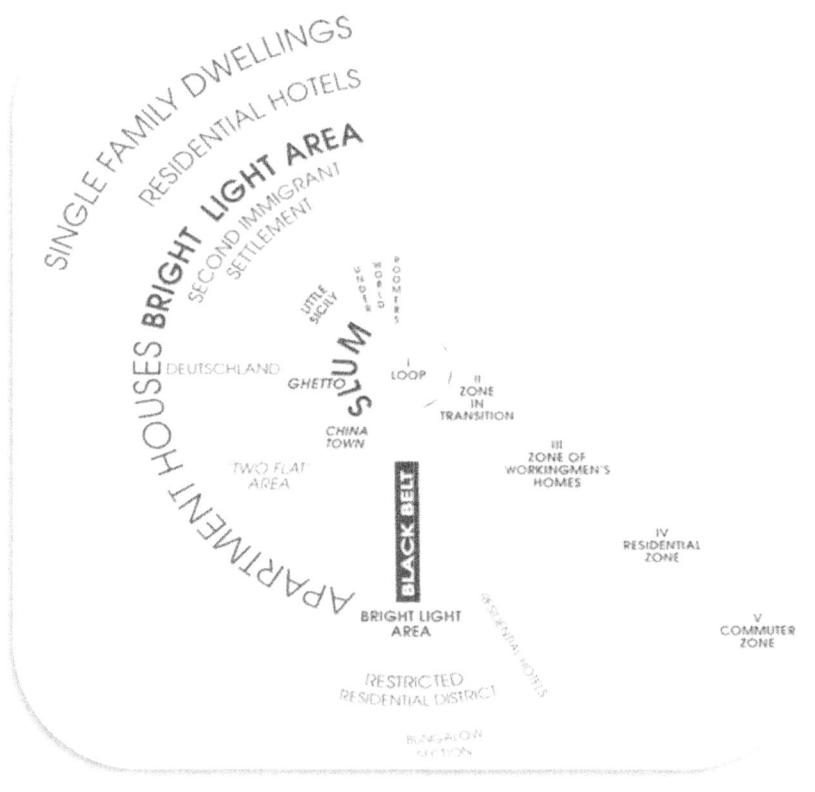

similar problem at a different time and continent.[31]

However, the policing and policing policies which were born in the UK were used in the USA, these policies survived the revolution and even after the revolution many of the UKs policing policies were continued, the Chicago model used the Chicago theories of crime coupled with the UKs policing policies, it can be defined as a type of hybrid crime and policing policy which was the forerunner to the modern USA crime and policing policies.

---

[31] https://cybergeo.revues.org/5332

Robert Park and Ernest Burgess

This also builds on the routine activities theory, the defensible spaces theory suggests that routine activity places may be regulated far more easily than the routine activities of persons, in criminology this theory suggests that places are easier to watch than people.

The research carried out by Park and Burgess involved detailed statistics and geographic maps, they researched the relationship between crime and selected urban social variables, the variable which they started with were poverty,

overcrowding and dilapidation. Further research by Shaw in 1927 found environmental association between crime and delinquency He framed the term or label, delinquency Shaw found that areas with more slums such as fringe districts where overcrowding was rife suffered with more crime, he also stated that districts or slums with high population of foreign and black residents who were poorly or unskilled workers suffered from a higher rate of crime. This research was also carried out in Boston and Philadelphia by Shaw and

McKay in 1942 also showed higher rates of crime where there was a high instance of population transition supported the claims of Park and Burgess that crime and delinquency producing social disorganisation.

Not based on the Chicago School but building on it Oscar Newman conducted research in 1972 which he claimed crime that a defensible space was a more rational theory, he claimed that if there was no way of the residents of an area to supervise the area they lived then crime would go unnoticed per se, i.e. high rise towers were no supervisory and only the people on any given floor could know what was going on in that area. Leaving for a scope (for unsupervised criminal behaviour), in the other areas of the block. He changed his theories in the 1980s however, due to widespread criticism of his research and findings.

The Chicago coined the term deprivation, this terms defines deprivation as being by researching the following:

- the basis of unemployment,
- children in low learning households,
- overcrowding, households lacking basic amenities,
- lack of cars,
- low educational attainment,
- mortality rates as a health measure.

Further research in the UK by the Social Exclusion Unit has said that a study of 20 of the most deprived estates in the UK found that 23 per cent of schools which were specifically for estates achieved no GCSEs at grades A to C, a significantly higher "failure" rate, also residents of estates were over ten times more likely to be the victims of crime.

Right Realism

Yet another school of thought, this school believed that crime was within the individual and not society as a whole, Right Realists saw crime as a result of the combination of a person's genetic makeup and their social environment. They claimed that because of a person's genetic predisposition some people would be inclined to engage in

criminality. They argued that this predisposition could be controlled through social conditioning in the family, in the school and other community activities. While it was suggested that lower class families and lone parents were the most likely to be involved in criminal activity, this did not explain white collar crime, and falters in its findings.

Right realists claimed that there needed to be tougher laws which should be enforced to the maximum, Right realists believed that crime was not due to a social structure but where social discipline was not used. This school of thought has not been without its critics, the main criticisms include, but not limited to the following;

• Crime is not limited to the streets, there are far more factors at play
• No accounting for white collar crime in their findings
• Focuses on individualistic crimes and not crimes to society or invisible crimes (insurance fraud etc.)
• The basis of Right Realism is a negative view of human nature (that people are naturally selfish and greedy).

Left idealists

Left idealists were in complete contrast to the right realists, they believed that the capitalists or high power individuals in society were responsible for the majority of the worst crimes within society (because the poor wanted what the rich had and it was their fault when the poor rebelled and tried to obtain those things). They had the opinion and beliefs that lower class individuals only committed crimes in retaliation against oppression from the elite. They had no wish to determine the causes of crime, they just wanted someone to blame.

"An idealist believes the short run doesn't count. A cynic believes the long run doesn't matter. A realist believes that what is done or left undone in the short run determines the long run." — Sydney J. Harris

Left Realism sees crime as a real problem for ordinary people and explains it through analysis social and economic relationships, and how some groups become marginalised.

They focus on victims as well as offenders, recognising crime is concentrated in the inner-city and sink housing estates. They did not focus on the crimes themselves, they were more interested in blame, however, this school faltered in their theories, the questions the left idealist theorists were asked the following questions in order to explain their theories;

- Which high power individuals within society were responsible for the burglaries and home invasions by default, the idealists believed this was rebelling against oppression.
- Explain why middle or lower class individuals were more like to attack other middle or lower class individuals, where were the high power individuals in this or why was it their fault.
- If the elite were responsible for the lower class crime then how could the idealists explain, rape, domestic abuse, in terms of rebellions against the elite?

White Collar Crime

Edwin Sutherland first coined the phrase "white collar crime" in the 1940s; this was to define crimes committed by so called, respectable people. This was to describe crimes which had they been committed by other offenders at this time, would have been classed as criminal and probably charged also. This was the beginning of criminalising behaviour of those in power and positions of power when partaking in criminal behaviour, such behaviour as; Insider dealing, money laundering, credit card fraud, insurance fraud, time share and pension fraud.

Insider Dealing

Insider dealing is a criminal offence; it is capable of a criminal sanction of up to 10 years in prison, and a fine of up to €10million euro.

Insider dealing can be defined as occurring when a person or parties have price sensitive information which is not generally available about a company's performance and deals in that information to make a profit.

1. Member of admin, management, board etc.
2. Holds capital.
3. Has access to the information,
4. Criminal activities.

IFCMP Act 2009 and the Market Abuse (Directive) Regulations 2005 defines information as precise and sensitive, it is not freely available information and it relates to the shares, etc. this information is not yet public and an investor would use in their decision to invest or information that could affect the prices of the securities.

Civil courts may direct the dealer (the person taking and using the information) to pay compensation to anyone who was not in information and lost money due to that.

Money laundering

Money laundering is a process whereby the proceeds of criminal means are concealed (drug trafficking, gun smuggling, corruption, etc.) and given the appearance of coming from legitimate sources. This is done by giving the illegal money the appearance of legitimacy and inserting it into the economy by.

1. Concealing or disguising the true nature of the property.
2. Converting, transferring, handling, acquiring, possessing or using the property; or
3. Removing the property from, or bringing the property into, the State.

The advent of the offshore bank accounts and Swiss bank accounts which were not only a tax haven but also free from patrolling by the Police helped to distinguish the source of the proceeds. One of the more famous havens was the Cayman Islands. Money laundering is an increasing concern for all Governments, especially because of its links to terrorism. It is vital that all countries sign up to combat money laundering, this international cooperation between police and financial agencies can go somewhat towards the fight against money laundering and terrorist financing.

Under Section 7(1) of the Criminal Justice (Money Laundering and Financing Terrorism) Act 2010

Criminal Sanctions for money laundering are up to 14 YEARS and/or a fine on indictment or 1 year summary and/or a fine of up to €5,000. All financial Institutions must report transactions over €15,000

Other forms of white collar crimes include:

1. Insurance fraud by insurance sellers and claimants
2. Credit card fraud
3. Customs fraud
4. Pension scheme fraud

5.   Time share and retirement home fraud.

White collar crimes are normally committed by less powerful businessmen and fraudsters, these types of financial frauds don't normally affect the economy negatively and also a higher rate of prosecutions.

Theories of Violent Crime

Fear of crime has been defined by Ferraro: (1995) *"an emotional response of dread or anxiety to crime or symbols that a person associates with crime."*

Fear of crime is not just the fear of violent to the person, it extend to the property, family and friends etc., it makes people feel vulnerable and in turn can cause an impact on a person's quality of life.

Murder

Murder is one of the greatest fears of most members of society; however it must be noted that although a heinous crime and socially unacceptable it is now an almost daily occurrence when as early as the 1980s to hear of a murder in Ireland drew breath of horror, nowadays it at best gets a "that's awful" or "what is the world coming to".

Murder is the most serious offence which can be perpetrated; it is an act which, if found guilty will find the offender getting a minimum sentence of life.

Murder can be defined as premeditated, or intentional with malice aforethought, (intention to kill and prepare for it) and manslaughter which is intentional or accidentally without malice aforethought, (no intention, no preparations), manslaughter can be voluntary (illegal, not self-defence etc.) or involuntary (kill another person while committing another crime such as burglary of robbery)

Gang Crime

Ireland and the UK shared on criminal family for decades, the Dundon Gang from Limerick Ireland had spent over 30 years living in London, here the families reputation as gang leaders was cemented in 2003 when Kenneth Snr was officially placed on Scotland Yard's most wanted, their MO was burglary and intimidation. All bar two of Kenneth's children followed in his footsteps into crime and John Dundon came to Ireland in 2007 and continued the family tradition of gangland violence, John was arrested and sentenced for the murder of Shane Geoghegan who was mistaken for John McNamara, his arch rival in 2008. Four out of the six Dundon children are incarcerated in Ireland for gangland violence.

The history of gangs

Gangs in the 50s and 60's in the UK and the USA were in the form of the Kray twins in the UK and the Mafia in the USA. These gangs were all about the money, this money came from protection rackets, prostitution and smuggling, and these feuds were also about control.

Gang Crime

Modern gangs

Modern gangs are more about "turf" about control of particular areas, it is about honour and respect, hits on rival gangs are often ordered due to one member feeling disrespected or dishonoured. It is also found that many young people enter gangs with the intent of finding where they belong, looking for the security and sense of belonging or an alternative to "family".

Theories of Criminal Behaviour

Can we discuss crime without asking the age old question: what causes it to occur? Criminal and forensic psychology is the study of why individuals commit crimes, the theories of what made them do the crime (psychologically) (Mens Rea, guilty mind) and why they behave (act) in certain ways (Actus Reus, guilty act).

By understanding why a person commits a crime, ways can be developed to control crime or rehabilitate the offender. There are many theories in criminology. Some theorists say that crime is relative to the individual; they believe that an individual weights the pros and cons and makes a conscious choice whether or not to commit a crime.

Others believe it is the community's responsibility to ensure that the residents do not commit crime by offering them a safe and secure place in which to live. Some theorists believe that some individuals have hereditary traits that will determine how they will react when put in certain hostile conditions. By studying these theories and applying them to individuals, it is hoped that psychologists can deter criminals from being recidivistic and help in their rehabilitation.

In Order to understand criminal behaviour we need to understand what factors are connected with or "cause" the criminals to do the crime. Gardaí, the Judiciary, the prison service and probationary services strive to understand the theories of crime and provide information. Knowing something about the factors associated with criminal behaviour, the characteristics of offender types, and the "causes" of crime provides information with which to:

- Pursue and investigate suspects
- Adjudicate defendants, determine the level of sentencing
- Manage offenders in correctional institutions, make parole and re-entry decisions, and to design crime prevention and crime control strategies.

Psychoanalysis

Psychoanalytic theorists and the origins of crime

Psychoanalysis

Henry Maudsley (1835–1918): Maudsley concluded that criminals were suffering from "moral degeneracy," a deficiency of moral sense. Sigmund Freud (1856–1939): Human behaviour can be explained by examining early childhood experiences. Sigmund Freud is the father of neuropsychological analysis and his theories formed the basis for future theorists, some to prove his finding and those who disproved many of his theories. Freud only ever worked with adults looking back on childhood experiences, he never worked with children. Therefore there could be problems with accuracy due to the human's inability to reproduce accurate memories or "eye witness testimony" (Munsterberg). Freud's insistence on sticking to the theories of the criminal behaviour stem from the childhood were quickly ruled out and caused a weakness in his theories. However, his three parts to the human "being" or "the personality" are still being used. Freud's theories suggest that we are driven by the EGO, the SUPER EGO and the ID.

The ID is the unconscious thought, the instant gratification, for instance, sex or violence, it's the theory of "if it feels good then do it". (Lester & Van Voorhis, cited in, Criminology: Theory, Research, and Policy; Gennaro Vito, Jeffrey Maahs)[32]

Superego, this can be described as your conscious, from moral reasoning, "lying is wrong" to self-reasoning or self-awareness "when I grow up I want to be just like mummy".

Ego: known as the "psychological thermostat" that regulates the wishes of the personal wishes of the id with the social restrictions of the superego.

---

[32] Vito. G, Maahs. J, 2011; Criminology: Theory, Research, and Policy. Jones & Bartlett

Freud's theories also claimed that Human nature is inherently antisocial, insofar as; Id: infants start life with antisocial drives; Superego: forms from experience; Ego: helps to negotiate demands for instant gratification with acceptable behaviour. If the ego is not strong enough to stabilise the demands of the ID and the SUPEREGO then behavioural deviation will follow. I.E. if a person's ID is stronger than their EGO, then this could give them a tendency to becoming a rapist in later life due to their having a stronger pleasure drive than SUPEREGO. Take for instance a psychopath, they are unable to process guilt and they have no ability to empathise with their victim, the SUPEREGO who is telling them they are doing something "wrong" simply not processed, they can commit the crime without the feelings of empathy or guilt needed to make them rethink their actions.

Sexual Offenders

Sexual offenders are typically seen as a similar group of offenders. However, it is well established nowadays that there is unlimited variety amongst sex offenders (Bartol & Bartol, 2011).

- type of sexual activity,
- age,
- background,
- attitudes,
- beliefs,
- personality,
- religion.

Also there are differences in the types of victims, the use of violence and the degree of planning. They rarely stop at sexual crimes and have been known to have an array of crimes they are charged with when arrested.

Adolescent males perpetrate 20-30% of all rapes, and 30-50% of all child molestations (Becker & Johnson, 2001). 70% of adolescent sex offenders come from two-parent homes, attend school and are successful, and don't suffer from any kind of mental disorder (Becker & Johnson, 2001). It is becoming more apparent that preadolescents (boys and girls) also commit sexual offences.

Sexual aggression can be observed in children as young as 3 or 4. A very large proportion of preadolescent girls carry out acts of sexual violence. Their behaviour is just as aggressive as that seen in boys. The victims of preadolescent offenders are typically very young (4-7) and the victim is known to the offender (sibling, friend, acquaintance). Very little is known about why such young children sexually offend.

Biological Theories of Crime

Rape

Acquaintance Rape ("date rape") is very common – as high as 60% of all rape cases. The UN has reported that sexual abuse of women and girls is rampant across many parts of the undeveloped world – e.g. Afghanistan, Saudi Arabia, Somalia, Chile, and India. In the western world, the U.S. has the highest incidence of rape.

The FBI reported 71,857 rapes in 2004 – 5% of all violent crime. 9% of reported rapes were committed against males and 1% is female-to-female rapes. The true figure however is vastly higher as most rapes go unreported, which makes it extremely difficult to obtain accurate figures. Just think about the abuse within the Catholic Church in Ireland and across the world and the incidence of prison rapes as well as the incidence of marital rape.

Data about perpetrators of rape crimes comes from convicted felons, which need to be considered in light of the fact that only 3% of reported rapes result in conviction. These individuals are a very unrepresentative sample.

Rapists tend to be young with 43% under 25 and 15%, under 15. 5% were under 15 (11% for all sexual offences). This appears to be a massive underestimation however, as other findings suggest at least 30% of rapes are committed by early adolescents (Cellini, 1995). A consistent finding is that rapists have continual and repeated violations of the law. Scully and Marola (1984) found that 82% of rapists had a prior criminal record. Only 23% had previously been convicted of a sexual offence.

Many rapists are unemployed and two-thirds are unmarried which is in contrast to paedophiles where two-thirds are married and most are employed. Large scale research studies (e.g. Black & Pettway, 2001) found that very few rapists reoffend sexually following release from prison. 1.3% of rapists were rearrested for another sex crime within 6 months of release (Langan et al., 2003). After three years, 5% of rapists were rearrested for another sex crime.

However, 41% were rearrested for a nonsexual crime after 3 years and 15% of these were for violent crimes not including rape or sexual offences. Rapists have been classified in terms of their perceptions of their crimes: Deniers and Admitters. Admitters are those who accept full responsibility for their actions and fully corroborate the account of their victim.

Deniers justify their rape behaviour by making the victim blameworthy and ultimately responsible. Their account of the rape incident typically differs considerably from that of the victim.

Five themes run through deniers justifications.

1. Women are seductresses,
2. Women really mean yes when they say no,
3. Most women relax and actually enjoy it,
4. Nice girls don't get raped.
5. Rape is a minor offence since the person is not physically hurt.[33]

Most deniers characterise the victim as the aggressor; as ultimately responsible because they didn't protest enough; and that she deep down wanted it to happen and greatly enjoyed it.

---

[33] CONVICTED RAPIST'S VOCABULARY OF MOTIVE EXCUSES AND JUSTIFICATIONS - Diana Scully and Joseph Marolla - https://www.d.umn.edu/~bmork/2306/readings/scullyandmarollis.htm

Biological Theories of crime

Adoption Studies: Studies that have been done with children reared by biological parents compared to their siblings or twins reared by adoptive parents in an attempt to demonstrate a genetic link to criminal behaviour. Results have been mixed.

Genetic - Twin Studies

- An 'MZ apart' study is when two monozygotic children have been brought up apart. If both turn out to be criminals then this would be support for the genetic explanation. The degree of similarity between two twins is known as the concordance rate. This rate can then be compared with dizygotic twins ('DZ together') who are brought up together
- Looking at a number of studies the average concordance rate is 55% for MZ twins and 17% for DZ twins (Bartol, 1999).

Genetic - Adoption Studies

- If a child who has criminal parents is adopted and later the child becomes a criminal then this will lend support to the genetic explanation.
- A study by Schulsinger (1972) found that only 3.9% of such children developed criminal tendencies. This was compared with control children (adopted children from non-criminal biological parents), where 1.4% became criminal. The small difference was not significant. The sample was large at 57, so there was a good prospect of detecting significance. The psychopathy was loosely defined as impulse-ridden behaviour.
- Crowe (1974) found that in a sample of 52 adopted children of imprisoned women; seven of them had at least one criminal conviction, by comparison with only one in a matched control group.
- Mednick et al (1987) found 14,000 adoptees amongst court convictions. Many had criminal biological parents (particularly strong relationship for sons and fathers). There was no

relationship in the types of crime committed. Improved social conditions reduced crime (going against the genetic explanation).

Autonomic Nervous System (ANS). Mednick's theory; that individuals who inherit a slower than normal autonomic nervous system learns to control aggressive or antisocial behaviour slowly or not at all. This leads to increased violence and criminal activity.

Criminaloid. One of three criminal types identified by Lombroso. The criminaloid is motivated by passion, and will commit criminal acts under the proper circumstances.

Determinism. In considering biological theories, determinism refers to the view that an individual's criminal lifestyle or actions is the direct result of genetic inheritance or biological predisposition. Soft determinism, as explained by Matza, examines the role of determinism, but also acknowledges that other factors, from environmental to choice, may be part of the equation. This assumes that behaviour is not completely and strictly determined by the individual's genetic or biological makeup.

Evolutionary Theory. A broad-based view that certain types of criminal behaviour are genetic and passed down from one generation to the next through evolutionary processes of natural selection and survival.

Gene-Based Evolutionary Theory. A general approach that suggests that the process of natural selection has resulted in criminal genetic tendencies that are passed down from generation to generation.

Insane Criminal. One of three criminal types identified by Lombroso. The insane criminal type includes idiots, imbeciles, epileptics, psychotics, and the mentally unstable. These criminals are unable to control their actions; however, they do not possess the stigmata or identifying characteristics of the born criminal.

Stigmata. Characteristics claimed by Lombroso that could be used to identify the "born criminal." They include things such as extra fingers or toes, large lips, receding chins, excessive skin wrinkles, and large monkey-like ears.

Intelligence and Learning in Criminology

Intelligence: capacity to act purposefully, think rationally and deal effectively with the environment.

Godard's perceptions of intelligence:

- Culture-bound concept: skills necessary for success in a culture
- Lombroso hypothesised that his criminals were "feebleminded", but there were no measure of intelligence
- Binet test: this was the first intelligence test. Used the concept of mental age: if the majority of children of a given age can complete a task, the task requires that mental age.
- Problem: MA does not change after mid-adolescence but chronological age does. Thus, using Binet's test, everyone would become feebleminded

Goddard's work was discredited

- It was until the 1970s that the issue of intelligence and crime was reconsidered by criminologists

- He tested children, compared mental age to chronological age

- 10-15 point gap between offenders and non-offenders: 100 v. 87

- More than 10% of prisoners are MR, while the percentage in the general population is less than 3%

- Is this because of social class differences between prisoners and the general population?

Studies of non-delinquent and delinquent adolescents matched for age, social class and ethnic groups also find an IQ difference, although not as large,

• Lower IQ scores are associated with higher recidivism among offenders

Crime addictions

(Peale. S, 1985) *"addictive experiences are potent modifiers of mood and sensation".* [34]

There is a common theory that the following characteristics of addictions include:[35]

- Tolerance - the need for more to produce the same effect.
- Withdrawal - distress after a period of non-engagement.
- Craving - distress associated with desire to re-engage.
- Salience - increasing importance of addiction in lifestyle.
- Conflict - increasing awareness of negative consequences.
- Relapse - reinstatement after a decision to stop or reduce.

Tolerance

As with any behaviour whether negative or positive the tolerance levels are key. A runner who runs one mile today may feel that one mile tomorrow is insufficient, they may need to run 1.1 miles to get the same emotional feelings from the run. This is the same with criminality, Criminals may become more and more tolerant to their own behaviour and the acts may need to increase in order to obtain the same desired effect.

Withdrawal

As with any addiction crime also has withdrawal symptoms. When a smoker stops smoking they may feel agitated, irritated and even upset

---

[34] PEELE, S.(1985) The Meaning of Addiction: Compulsive Experience and its Interpretation. Lexington MA, Lexington Books.
[35] Hodge. J; http://www.offenders-anonymous.org.uk/section.html?secpath=01.08.&pgid=1

to a point of anger or fear. They may feel that the feelings are so intense that the only way to relieve them is to smoke a cigarette. This is true for other addictions, such as crime, undertaking another "job" may relieve those withdrawal symptoms.

Craving

When the body has a craving, there is a longing, a longing to commit the crime, smoke the cigarette, run the extra mile. When the craving becomes stronger the withdrawal symptoms in turn increase the craving for the activity, for instance, I want, I want I want.

Salience

Salience, when not committing the crimes the offender may be daydreaming about it, planning it or even executing it in their minds

Euphoria / relief / mood regulation

The feel good feeling an addicts gets when they "give in" to their cravings and partake in the behaviour i.e. smoking, drinking, running, crime. They get a "feel good" response from the actions.

Conflict

When a person undertakes behaviour they "know" they should not be undertaking, they often feel inner conflict, they know what they are doing is wrong, and yet they continue with that behaviour.

Relapse

As with any addiction the person may feel that they will "give up or stop" the addiction or behaviour, they may feel that it is not legally, morally or personally right to be partaking in the behaviour so they take the decision to stop.

However, like some addictions crime is incredible difficult to stop and offenders regularly reoffend or relapse after deciding not to do it again.

Recognising criminal addictions

How is it possible to recognise addicted offenders? The characteristics are a starting point, the factors defined above, if a burglar commits more and more elaborate break-ins, and in essence the appearance of a motivational factor is evident from the details it could be discussed how the offender is addicted to committing the act rather than any other reason, in essence it could be said that if addicted to crime offenders are identified then the rehabilitation could be more successful.

It may also be evident in incarceration facilities when offenders are reluctant to be released, as they know that they will reoffend and have a personal knowledge of their addiction, creating conflict, and they may have made a concerted decision not to reoffend while when released they relapse because the craving is too overwhelming.

For some types of offence, for example joyriding or shoplifting, its role may be minimal since the offence behaviour itself is capable of frequent expression, while for other types of offence, such as certain sexual offences, fantasy may be the central component driving the offending through the mechanism of tolerance.

A Theoretical Model of Behaviour Addictions for Addictive Offenders adapted by Brown (1997)

Specialisation in a single offence, or a narrow range of similar offences. It is unlikely that anyone can be addicted to crime as a whole or to a range of criminal activities which might be expected to provide widely differencing subjective emotional experiences. Individual vulnerabilities of the person involved similar to those identified for addictions – for example, poor relationships and a restricted range of easily-accessible rewarding activities.

Powerful emotional reaction experienced by the individual in association with the criminal act which is mood-changing – colloquially, a strong 'buzz' for the individual. Increasing salience of the criminal activity so that, even when it is not being committed, it is being planned or fantasised about and all of life, thinking, feeling and behaviour is dominated by and organised around the next opportunity to offend.

Positive feedback loops promoting increasing and repeated offending, such as;

- conflict narrowing the range of easily-accessible alternative rewarding activities,
- tolerance escalating the risks to be taken to achieve the same escape,
- withdrawals leading to restlessness and irritability when offending is not possible,
- and relief offending arising out of the need to block despair and guilt from the last offence by beginning preoccupation with the next.

Cycles of criminal activity – corresponding to cycles of need to use the criminal activity to manage hedonic tone in the offender. Offenders often have;

Addictions

- Low self-esteem – subjective feelings of loss of control, unable to cut down offending or be abstinent.
- Rituals before or after offending – a series of routines or chains of stimuli, responses, actions which seem to build up or break down arousal.
- Disconnection from normal flow of mental life – offence feels it is being committed in a 'time capsule' apart from ordinary life.
- Patterns of reoffending which look like relapse in the addictions – i.e., involves fantasies stimulated by relapse-provoking situations which become progressively more extreme and dominant as the offence is approached.
- Occasional reinstatement phenomena – even after many years of remission, a rapid reversion to the frequency and intensity of offending which was characteristic of offending at its height, perhaps many years before.

Media and Crime

Is Crime distorted in the media? What are the sources of the stories which claim to be research based or what truth is there behind the masses of criminal stories and statistics which we reading our papers and online news sources and feeds every day?

The Media Representation of Crime

The media does not care about statistics and qualitative or quantitative research, it is concerned with selling papers, magazines, and moves, the media's portrayal of crime and statistical analysis of crimes should be "taken with a pinch of salt" when discussing crimes and criminal statistics.

Are newspapers and magazines feed societies fear of crime and in essence creating a catch 22 or loop situation? Skogan (1987) stated that

"a high level of fear of crime often appears not only in those who are more likely to be victimised, such as the poor and those living in inner city areas, but also those who enjoy comparatively low levels of recorded victimisation, such as women and the elderly".

The statistics give an insight into the portrayal of crime, and shockingly over 75% of those who were asked about what they had just read or seen in the news believed that the media's interpretation of the crimes was accurate. Graber (1980)

The effects of this media portrayal of crime has a worrying reaction from many members of society, such as removing and withdrawing from society, not going out as much, taking excessive precautions in safety in areas know to suffer with excessive criminal activity, explain that *"for those fearing victimisation, each excursion beyond the relative safety of home is like walking through a minefield – at any moment, a purse may be snatched, a body assaulted, a sense of dignity affronted". Box et al. (1988)*

Generally, the media are seen as exaggerating the risks associated with crime and criminal behaviours and this is believed to be done in an effort to increase sentences and make punishments harsher.

Statistics for media coverage

- Crimes of violence are disproportionately covered.
- Murder: accounts for 1/3rd of all reports.
- Burglary received less coverage than murder
- 64.5% of newspaper crime stories are violent, despite only 6% of all convicted crimes being violent
- Fatal crime accounted for 38-53% of crime stories.

From the above statistics it can be seen that fatality, killing, horrific deaths and murder sell stories, as does the medias need to ensure we are aware of the offenders "social status, i.e. poor, unemployed, ethnicity and male etc."

The media tend to focus on sensationalist, prurient, and moralistic stories reflects the desires of the general public, the old adage rings true, *"believe half of what you see, and none of what you hear".* The media can heighten fear and perceptions amongst the general public; it can also be seen to enforce notions of the theories of crime, by using the following;

Labelling Theory:

- The media establishes stereotypes and social beliefs of criminality, through labelling those are criminals, or criminal types the media establishes and reinforce labels.

Deviancy Theory

- The media identifies the types of deviant groups which are then reinforced by alienation. Fear of those deviants are then portrayed and amplified.

Strain Theory

- The media, and in particular advertising, is central to the establishment of people's goals: economic goals.

Chapter four – The emergence of the Irish Legal System

The Irish Legal System

What is "Law"?

It is possible to describe law as the body of official rules and regulations, generally found in constitutions, legislation, judicial opinions, etc., they are used to govern a society and to control the behaviour of members within society, so the law is a recognised instrument of social control.

Explanation; Every country needs a legal system so that people can live in peace and free from worry about being attacked or imprisoned, stolen from or harmed emotionally or physically. A legal system is a guide for a group of people, cultures, and societies to live within a municipal system. The law governs how society behaves towards each other. The aim and objective of laws and regulations is to include protecting the rights of all citizens.

Brehon Law

Irish History has had a great effect on the laws of the land. Ireland has a history of bloody invasions and tyrannical reign over its people, from the Viking invaders, to the Norman invasions to the British conquests, none more so than the British invasion of the 17th Century when the old Brehon (the old name in for lawgiver) legal system was abolished by Queen Elizabeth the 1st, claiming it was barbaric and unreasonable and even barbarous. The Brehon system was overseen by representatives, these were taken from the community, they were; the chief, poet, historian, landowner, bishop, professor of literature, professor of law, a noble, and a lay vicar, it was these representatives that made and changed the laws, these laws covered every conceivable aspect of daily life in Ireland, it referred to the behaviours within each community and each community could have different laws.

The richer the person the more legal standing they would have within the community, this was also held to be classless, as the Kings and High Kings would have to adhere to the laws of the Brehons the same as any menial labourer. Richer members of society were held more accountable for their actions than a poorer, if a rich farmer stole a cow from a poor farmer, his fine would be a lot more severe than if the poor farmer had stolen from the rich.

In Brehon times in Ireland women were equal to men, they were Queens, led their armies into battles, they were poets, doctors and were able to bring cases against other people, it was the reign of Queen Elizabeth 1st ironically that led to the ending of Brehon laws and with them the rights of women.

An example of some of the strange and abstract Brehon laws which were in existence, (taking into account most of these laws were written down by St Patrick and when people still lived in mud huts and life revolved around the commune)

Examples of Brehon Laws; how people interacted with each other.

- February first is the day on which husband and wife may decide to walk away from the marriage.
- When you become old the family must provide you with one oatcake a day plus a container of sour milk. They must bathe you every 20th night and wash the head every Saturday. Seventeen sticks of firewood is the allotment for keeping you warm.
- No fools, drunks or female scolds are allowed in the doctor's house when a patient is healing there. No bad news to be brought and no talking across the bed. No grunts of pigs or barking of dogs outside.
- A husband who through listlessness does not go to his wife in her bed must pay a fine.
- If a pregnant woman craves a morsel of food and her husband withholds it though stinginess or neglect he must pay a fine.
- Whoever comes to the door you must feed him and care for him with no questions asked.

Explanation; the Brehons, or 'brithemuin', were like the judges or jurists of today, however we can describe Brehon's as being similar to mediators. Their role was to ensure a stable society by a series and system of fines, there was no prison time, nor corporal (physical) punishment, if you behaved against the rules you paid a fine, it was as simple as that. A person could go to the home and demand that you pay then what you owe them and you could not leave the home until it was paid, if you injured someone you had to pay their way until they healed, food etc. This was originally thought to be a system of barbaric rules, however on investigation in modern times Brehon law is deemed to be one of the most sophisticated of its time anywhere in Europe which was based on the theory of natural law (fair, just and reasonable) whereby people were put before property no matter what the class or how much wealth you had.

Sources of Law in Ireland

The Four sources of Irish law

1. The Constitution
2. European Community law
3. Common law
4. Legislation

The sources of law in Ireland consist of constitutional, statute law, common law and EU law. The highest law in the State is the Constitution of Ireland, however this law gives way to the Supremacy of EU law, from which all other law derives its authority. The Republic has a common-law legal system with a written constitution that provides for a parliamentary democracy with an elected president, a separation of powers, which is the cornerstone of Irish law.

Source 1 - European Community Law

Ireland has a Common Law Legal System with a written constitution, this constitution provides that the Oireachtas may use statutory instruments in order to implement European Union law, this power derived from the *European Communities Act, 1972,* (as amended) which stated that statutory instruments have effect as if they were primary legislation.[36]

Ireland's membership of the European Community requires that Ireland accommodates EC legislation in its entirety, therefore, Ireland agrees to the Supremacy of EC law. Ireland must implement EC legislation, while taking account of Irelands Constitution. The European Union is supported by five principle institutions.

---

[36] **European Communities Act, 1972** http://www.irishstatutebook.ie/eli/1972/act/27/enacted/en/html

Sources of Law in Ireland

1. The European Commission;
2. The Council of European Union;
3. The European Parliament;
4. The European Court of Justice;
5. The European Court of Auditors

The Doctrine of Supremacy

The case of *Van Gend en Loos, [1963] ECR1*,[37] provided for a *"new legal order"* and established that EC law has supremacy over national laws. This was further restated in the case of *Costa v Enel, [1964] ECR 585*[38] which meant that the EC Treaty was supreme to National law and all treaty provisions were binding on all states and their citizens. As Ireland has a written constitution whereby it is stated in *Article 15.2.1 of the Irish Constitution that: The sole power of making law is given to Oireachtas. Explicitly states that "no other" legislative authority has power to make laws for the State."* This meant Ireland had to hold a referendum in order to amend the Constitution to allow for EC supremacy.

Article 15.2.1;

This amendment states where there is a conflict between European Community Law and Domestic Law, European Community law prevails and provisions of European Community law can be enforced before National Courts.

The laws of the EC derive from treaties.

---

[37] Judgment of the Court, Van Gend & Loos, Case 26-62 (5 February 1963)
http://www.cvce.eu/en/obj/judgment_of_the_court_van_gend_loos_case_26_62_5_february_1963-en-4b81dcab-c67e-44fa-b0c9-18c48848faf3.html
[38] Judgment of the Court of 15 July 1964. Flaminio Costa v E.N.E.L.
http://curia.europa.eu/juris/liste.jsf?language=en&jur=C,T,F&num=C-6/64&td=ALL

Sources of Law in Ireland

The European Community Treaties

1957 – The Treaty of Rome (the founding treaty)

1972 - Treaty of Accession -Brussels

1987 - The Single European Act (to remove trade barriers)

1993 - The Maastricht Treaty (creation of EU citizenship and EU Currency)

1997 - The Amsterdam Treaty (creation of jobs within the EU, this Treaty set out plans to be implemented by each member to tackle unemployment throughout the EU)

2001- The Nice Treaty (set out the division of power within the EU for each member country).

2009 – The Lisbon Treaty (Treaty of the Functioning of the EU) (recognised each countries responsibility to the Human Rights Act and made it legally binding on member Countries, it made responsibility more transparent, i.e. accountability for each countries actions and the impact it has on the EU). These treaties are the primary source of EC law, however on a day to day basic Regulations and Directives are the pieces of legislation which are called Secondary legislation.

2012 - European Fiscal Compact Treaty

Primary Law

Treaties are the starting point for EU law and are known in the EU as primary law.

Secondary Law

The body of law that comes from the principles and objectives of the treaties is known as secondary law; and includes regulations, directives, decisions, recommendations and opinions.

Article 249 of the EC Treaty states that the *"European Parliament acting jointly with the Council, the Council and the Commission shall make regulations and issue directives, take decisions, make recommendations or deliver opinions"*[39]

Laws approved by the institutions of the EC through the procedures defined within the Treaties are known as secondary legislation.

Article 249 states that "it is the responsibility of the EC Institutions to enact secondary legislation.

These secondary legislations are:

Regulations

A regulation shall have general application. It shall be binding in its entirety and directly applicable in all Member States. EC Regulations are directly binding in all Member States. Member States are required to introduce procedures for their implementation, such as penalties or fines. Regulations are binding in their entirety, no member Country can decide if there are areas or objectives of the Regulation they wish to enact. Each member Country has to abide by it in its entirety (completely)

Directives

Directives are binding *"as the result to be achieved, upon each Member State to which it is addressed, but shall leave to the national authorities the choice of form and methods."*

---

[39] Treaty establishing the European Community (Nice consolidated version) Part Five: Institutions of the Community Title I: Provisions governing the institutions http://eur-lex.europa.eu/LexUriServ/LexUriServ.do?uri=CELEX:12002E249:EN:HTML

Sources of Law in Ireland

(Example: EC Directives are binding on all Member States as to the <u>objectives to be achieved within a certain time limit</u>. But they are not binding in their entirety; this means it is up to each Country to enact legislation to give effect to the directives <u>intentions</u>, keeping their own Countries requirements, i.e. a regulation for a set minimum wage in every EC Country would not be viable. For instance, if a set minimum wage was introduced into Europe as €4.50 per hour, and this was directly binding on all member states, then this could cause a lot of hardship in some Countries. I.e. €4.50 per hour may be a wage that is sufficient in one Country but definitely not in Ireland, where the cost of living is so much higher, this is why the set minimum wage in Europe is a Directive, each Country has the ability to set its own minimum wage according to the cost of living. In Ireland it is presently €9.25 per hour, nonetheless it <u>MUST</u> have a minimum wage, that's the <u>purpose</u> of the directive).

Decisions

Decisions are binding in their entirety (*Completely*), on those persons/bodies/Countries that the Decisions are addressed, be it a Member State, a Country, an organisation or an individual. They do not need to be implemented into National Law.

Recommendations

Recommendations have no binding force. Recommendations are not binding, but express the Councils or Commission's view on policy, to the Member States or to the individuals to which they are addressed. Whilst not legally binding, they have political and moral significance and can be preliminary requirements to subsequent mandatory rules.

Opinions

Opinions have no binding force. Opinions are not binding, but express the Councils or Commission's view on policy to the Member States or to the individuals to which they are addressed. Whilst not legally binding, they have political and moral significance.

Sources of law

Source 2 - The Irish Constitution

The primary source of law in Ireland until Ireland joined the EC was the Irish Constitution.

Bunreacht na hÉireann, 1937

The Constitution is a positive source of rights for Irish citizens, it confirms that the State is obliged to protect citizen's rights; this is done by enacting legislation if necessary. All other sources must be _"constitutional"_ otherwise it will be repugnant to the Irish state and can be challenged before the courts. _Crotty V An Taoiseach (1987)._

Article 15.2.1 of the Irish Constitution states: The sole power of making law is given to Oireachtas (everyone in the Dáil, Fianna Fail Fine Gael, and Labour etc.). Explicitly states that "no other legislative authority has power to make laws for the State."

Crotty v. An Taoiseach: The Supreme Court which found that Ireland could not ratify the Single European Act unless the Irish Constitution was first changed to permit its ratification

Article 25 of the Irish Constitution states that: _"The President must sign a Bill into law."_

Article 25.2.1 of the Irish Constitution states: _"that the President must sign such a Bill into law not earlier than the fifth and not later than the seventh day after the date in which it is presented to him"._

Article 50 of the Constitution of Ireland allowed all laws that had been in force in the Irish Free State prior to its coming into force on 29 December 1937 to continue to have force, (_meaning any UK laws which were enacted and not repugnant (not going against the core principles of the Irish Free State)_ before the new constitution was enacted were still binding law. There laws introduced by the

Sources of law

Constitution are called Articles, some of the major rights afforded by the Constitution are, the right to life, the right to assembly, the right to fair procedures, the right to a family life, to name a few.

The Irish Constitution was enacted by a popular plebiscite (*a vote of the common people*) held on 1 July 1937, and came into force on 29 December 1937. (*The Constitution is a written document which governs how Ireland should be run; it documents the rights, privileges and responsibilities of the Irish citizens and State*). The Irish Constitution can only be amended by referendum (*vote*) of the people (*by plebiscite or the common man*).

Changing the Constitution

A proposal to amend the Constitution is introduced into Dáil Éireann, and if passed by the Dáil, it is then put to the people for a referendum vote. If the referendum passes and the people agree to the changes to the Constitution, the President then signs the referendum bill into law. The president can refer any bill to the Supreme Court under Article 26 of the constitution for clarification of any terms which may be ambiguous (*unclear*) or repugnant (*distasteful, objectionable, or offensive*) before signing the bill into legislation or statute law.

Fundamental personal rights guaranteed under the Irish constitution

The Irish Constitution confers rights on Irish citizens, these rights are fundamental (no one take them away from you), they are broken down further into enumerated (*written down*) and unenumerated (unwritten, *the language, history, and structure of the constitution, or cases interpret it. It can also be defined as an inferred right.*).

Article 40.3 of the Irish Constitution refers to and accounts for the recognition of unenumerated rights.

Sources of law

Unenumerated rights

An example of an unenumerated right is the Right to Privacy. The Constitution does not precisely state a right to privacy. This unenumerated right protects a citizens against certain kinds of intrusion by persons or bodies , a citizen's private written communications and telephone conversations cannot be deliberately and unjustifiably interfered with (*save in accordance with the law (except when a citizen is breaking the law*)) *Kennedy V. Ireland*

Enumerated rights (some samples)

Article 40.1 of the Constitution

All citizens shall, as human persons, be held equal before the law. This shall not be held to mean that the State shall not in its enactments have due regard to differences of capacity, physical and moral, and of social function.

Article 41.1° of the Constitution

The State recognises the Family as the natural primary and fundamental unit group of Society,

Article 42.1 of the Constitution

The State acknowledges that the primary and natural educator of the child is the Family and guarantees to respect the inalienable right and duty of parents to provide, according to their means, for the religious and moral, intellectual, physical and social education of their children.

Sources of law

Article 43.1.1 of the Constitution

The State acknowledges that man, in virtue of his rational being, has the natural right, antecedent to positive law, to the private ownership of external goods.

Article 43.1.2 of the Constitution

The State accordingly guarantees to pass no law attempting to abolish the right of private ownership or the general right to transfer, bequeath, and inherit property.

Article 44.1 of the Constitution

[40]The State acknowledges that the homage of public worship is due to Almighty God. It shall hold His Name in reverence, and shall respect and honour religion.

---

[40] http://polyglotlegend.blogspot.ie/2016/

Sources of law

Source 3 - Common Law

After the abolishment of the Irish Brehon laws, Ireland was governed by what was then the English system of Common Law. The then Queen, Elizabeth I, wanted a uniform legal system, Common law was not just used by the English ruling sovereignty, this type of law originated with the Normans.

 Common law builds up over time, added to by the legislature (*statutes are presumed to add to, not alter, existing law*) and by precedent.

Common law is the process whereby a body of laws arises from precedent (*what went before, let it stand*) the decisions in previous cases are binding on future cases of the same standing (*materially similar in nature*).

Precedent also known as *"the doctrine of binding precedent"* is also known as *"Stare Decisis"* (*stand by the decision*) there are many translations for stare decisis but in plain English it means, a decision of a higher court binds all lower courts.

The doctrine of precedent means that a judge is bound to apply a decision from an earlier case to the facts of the case before them provided, among other conditions, that there is no material difference between the cases

The decision in court is divided into two distinct parts, firstly the "ratio decidendi" (*the reason for the decision, the reason for the guilty or not guilty verdict*) and "obiter dictum/dicta" (*something said by the way, something the judge may have said while summing up*), such as, in a recent Monaghan District Court hearing the Judge said that he would not be granting orders against debtors, *"because the banks were not negotiating with debtors to come to an agreement"* (*Ratio Decidendi*), and the banks can "*go whistle for their money*" (*obiter dictum*)). It must be noted that the obiter dictum is not binding; the ratio decidendi is binding, it creates the precedent which binds lower courts. However, the obiter may be <u>persuasive</u> (*taken into consideration*)

The system of Common law in Ireland is by and for a successful one, there are those who advocate that it is staunch and unfair, others who say it is very far too strict and judges are not allowed to use their discretion when cases are significantly similar yet the circumstances are different. Others believe that helps those to have some idea of how their case will go, what the outcome may be, therefore making for a plan of action as to the outcome of their own case.

(**Explanation:** *Common law was the decisions of Judges which was written down and the decisions then recorded in the court journals. These judgments were then used so that all law in the law was "Common" or the same everywhere in the Country; this ensured that the law was consistent. Common law precedent, (previous decisions of higher courts which were binding on all lower courts) may have been overturned by a higher court, i.e. the High Court may overturn a decision of the Circuit Court. Therefore, it is important that the legal representative knows the status of any precedent which may affect their client, this is why there are searches done in court journals.*)

Stare Decisis

The doctrine (principle) of Judicial Precedent - *stare decisis et non quieta movere* (*stare decisis*) (*stand by the decision and do not unsettle the established*) or the *Doctrine of Stare Decisis* is a doctrine whereby a judge must stand by the decision of a ruling in a superior court in a previously determined case. I.e. the High Court must follow decisions

Sources of law

of the Court of Appeal, which in turn must follow decisions of the Supreme Court. This principle ensures fair and just sentences which do not alter over millennia, and it recognises a fair and democratic society, which needs laws that rarely alter over time. (*There can be an argument for and against stare decisis, not changing with a modern time may in fact cause unfairness.*)

Ratio Decidendi

This is the binding part of the decision, or the reason for the decision, such as the reason the accused is sentenced to two years in prison is because all of the evidence against them, including CCTV, witness statements and admission of guilt. This is different from the Obiter Dicta, (something said along the way which does not form part of the decision). The Ratio Decidendi is the binding part of the decision which will bind future cases which are similar.

Obiter Dicta

This is something which is said by the judge either in his sentencing statement or decision. Such as the statement Obiter from *Judge Patrick Clyne* when he said he was sick of women *"treating men like sperm banks" and behaving "like black widow spiders"* this did not form any part of his decision, or the reason for it.[41]

---

[41] http://www.independent.ie/irish-news/judge-turns-his-anger-on-black-widows-25956439.html

Sources of law

Source 4 - Acts of the Oireachtas or Legislation

There are two types of Legislation in Ireland

1. Primary legislation

2. Secondary legislation

Primary Legislation

Article 15.2.1 of the Irish Constitution states: The sole power of making law is given to Oireachtas. Explicitly states that "no other" legislative authority has power to make laws for the State." [42]

The sole and exclusive power (*no other bodies or states can make laws for Ireland*) of making laws for the State is vested in the Oireachtas (*Parliament*) subject to the obligations of European Union Membership as provided in the Constitution of Ireland. The Oireachtas consists of the President and two Houses, Dáil Éireann (*House of Representatives*) and Seanad Éireann (*Senate*).

Legislation otherwise known as Statute law is made either, by the legislature as primary legislation, or by some other body in exercise of law-making powers delegated by the legislature, known then as *delegated or subordinate legislation.* All Legislation in Ireland has its beginnings as a Bill (*a draft of the proposed law*), this Bill starts as either a private members Bill (*rare in Ireland, these Bills are introduced into the Oireachtas or Seanad by a member of the government, "<u>these rarely pass</u>"*) and public members bills. (*the most common type, these are bills that would affect the populous, or the greatest amount of members of the pubic and introduced by government bodies*). Bills can

---

[42]http://www.irishstatutebook.ie/en/constitution/

Sources of law

be introduced in either the Dáil or Seanad. (*Normally the Dáil*) There are five stages to a bill becoming legislation.

Once the Bill is passed the Taoiseach presents a vellum copy (*calf skin*) of the Bill prepared in the Office of the Houses of the Oireachtas to the President for signature and declaration as a law.

Delegated/Secondary legislation

When a bill becomes law it becomes and Act, this act, then confers powers on the relevant minister to make changes or amendments to the act, this means that parts inside the act can be changed without the act itself being changed, therefore, saving Government time, notwithstanding the financial savings, of not having to introduce a new piece of legislation.

This is called delegated legislation. Delegated legislation means that a government or state body (*i.e. Government agencies, Minister for Health, Minister for Transport etc.*) can make changes to existing laws, in order to implement the requirements of legislation with the relevant authority.

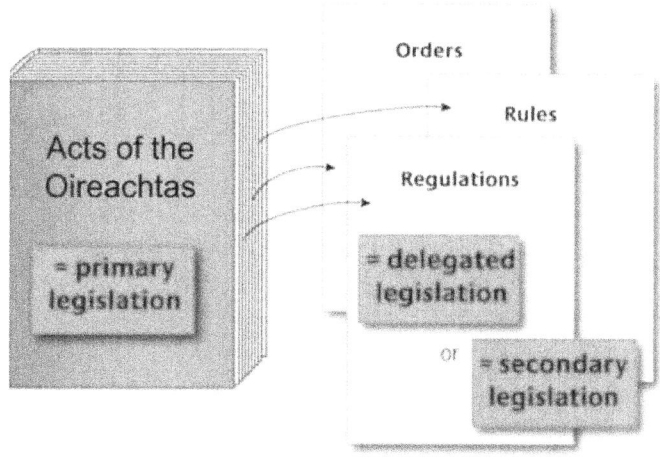

Sources of law

Secondary legislation, in the form of Statutory Instruments, is governed by the *Statutory Instruments Act 1947*.[43] There are five main types of statutory instrument *orders, regulations, rules, bye-laws and schemes*. Delegated legislation is a practical way to avoid overloading the Oireachtas.

Example of an Order:

The Road Traffic Act 2004:[44] The Manager of a City or County Council can reduce the speed limit on a road undergoing road works for a stated period of time by executive order under powers available to him/her under *the Road Traffic Act 2004. Road Traffic Act 2004: Road Traffic (Speed Limits) (County Borough of Dublin and County of Dublin) (Amendment) Regulations, 1992.* This authorised traffic on the M1, M7, M11 and M50 to travel at 113 km/h where signposted. This was extended to motorways in general *by the Road Traffic Act, 1994.* A minimum speed limit of 30 mph (48 km/h) had previously been set in 1974 through the *Local Government (Roads and Motorways) Act, 1974*

"That's not how you submit Pleadings to this Court."

---

[43] Statutory Instruments Act, 1947 http://www.irishstatutebook.ie/1947/en/act/pub/0044/

[44] The Road Traffic Act 2004 http://www.irishstatutebook.ie/2004/en/act/pub/0044/

Example of a Statutory Instrument

Sale of Goods and Supply of Services Act 1980: This legislation governs contracts for the sale of goods and supply of services to consumers. The Act provides that goods must be of merchantable quality, fit for their purpose and as described.

Associated Statutory Instruments:

Unfair Terms in Consumer Contracts; *European Communities (Unfair Terms in Consumer Contracts) Regulations 1995, (S.I. No. 27 of 1995). European Communities (Unfair Terms in Consumer Contracts) (Amendment) Regulations 2000 (S.I. No. 307 of 2000)*[45]

*(**Explanation:** Delegated or Secondary Legislation. Some may be referred to as Statutory Instruments, Rules, Regulations or Orders. They are used to specify requirements which were not inserted into the primary legislation, or statutes, such as commencement dates, how much a particular fine is etc. SI's allow the provisions of the acts to be brought into force without the Oireachtas having to pass a new Act therefore saving time and money as there are over 800 amendments, SI's, Orders or Regulations every year this would mean that the Oireachtas (Parliament) would not have time to run the Country if they were to bring in over 800 new Acts per year.)*

---

[45] European Communities (Unfair Terms in Consumer Contracts) (Amendment) Regulations 2000 (S.I. No. 307 of 2000) http://www.irishstatutebook.ie/eli/2000/si/307/made/en/print

Chapter Five – England and Wales Legal system

46

The English Legal System

The legal system in England is similar to Ireland; this is due to the fact that the Irish legal system originates in the UK.

Summary or indictable offences

Offences in England can be classified as Summary and Indictable; the trial depends how serious the offence is. Schedule 1 to the Interpretation Act 1978 provides that:

- indictable offence (serious offence) means an offence which, if committed by an adult, is triable on indictment, whether it is exclusively so triable or triable either way;
- summary offence means an offence which, if committed by an adult, is triable only summarily (less serious).

---

46 Domesday Book, illustration from William Andrews's Historic Byways and Highways of Old England, 1900.

The classification is an essential element in the process of deciding where an offence is to be tried, i.e. via a summary trial in a magistrates' court or a trial on indictment in the Crown Court. All common law offences are indictable, as are offences created by statute if the statute specifies a penalty to be imposed following trial on indictment.

In order to understand the reasons for the hierarchy of laws in the English Legal System one has first to appreciate the different institutions and their role in the law-making process

The three branches of government in England and Wales are:

- The Legislature
- The Executive
- The Judiciary

The Separation of Powers

The separation of powers is a fundamental principle in English law.

1. each branch of the state has separate and independent powers and areas of responsibility
2. the aim of the separation of powers is to establish a system of checks and balances; each branch controls the other two

John Locke (1690) – "if the same person has the power to make laws and execute them, they may exempt themselves from the laws they make and use the law to their own private advantage"

The Rule of Law

The rule of law, was popularised by AV Dicey in 1885, the Rule of law implies absolute supremacy of law. It guarantees that an individual can ascertain with reasonable certainty what legal powers are available to the government if an individual's rights are infringed. It does not exempt the officials and others from the duty of obedience to the law which governs other citizens or from jurisdiction of ordinary tribunals.

Article 6 - European Convention on Human Rights ("ECHR")

In the determination of his civil rights and obligations or of any criminal charge against him, everyone is entitled to a fair and public hearing within a reasonable time by an independent and impartial tribunal established by law. Judgment shall be pronounced publicly by the press and public may be excluded from all or part of the trial in the interest of morals, public order or national security in a democratic society, where the interests of juveniles or the protection of the private life of the parties so require, or the extent strictly necessary in the opinion of the court in special circumstances where publicity would prejudice the interests of justice.

How the law is made in England and Wales

In the England and Wales, both civil and criminal, is made in two ways:

- by an act of parliament. This is known as statute law;
- by the judgment of judges. This is known as common law.

All Acts start life as a Bill

A Bill is a proposal for a new law, or a proposal to change an existing law which is presented for debate before Parliament. A Bill can start in the House of Commons or the House of Lords, all Acts must be approved in both the House of Lords and the House of Commons before being enacted into law.

Bill proposals are made by

- The government
- Individual MPs or Lords
- Private individuals or organisations

Types of Bills

Public Bills are the most common type of bills and are usually proposed by the Government, these apply to the general population (e.g. Change to the speed limits on national roads, i.e. A5)

Private Members Bills are Public Bills introduced by MPs and Lords who aren't government ministers; only minority become law; may affect legislation indirectly by drawing attention to specific issues

Private Bills are usually promoted by organisations (e.g. local authorities or private companies) to give themselves powers beyond the general law;

Hybrid Bills are a mix the characteristics of Public and Private Bills; changes to the law proposed by a Hybrid Bill are of national importance but affect one part of the UK or a significant for a particular group or individual (e.g. Channel Tunnel Bills

The Legislative Process

First Reading

This is the formal introduction of the Bill into the House of Commons.

Second Reading

Main debate on Bill's principles (voted, can be defeated)

Committee Stage

Clause by clause consideration of the Bill by a select committee (amendments added)

Report Stage

Committee reports suggested amendments back to the House of Commons, only amendments are discussed, new amendments may be added)

Third Reading

Final debate on the Bill

The Process in the House of Lords

All stages are repeated BUT if the House of Lords votes against the Bill, it can go back to the House of Commons and become law if the House of Commons passes it for the second time (rare occurrence)

Royal Assent

A formality - normally Acts of Parliament come into force at midnight after receiving the Royal Assent

Sources of Law English law

Statute Law

Also referred to as Acts of Parliament, or primary legislation, such as the Road Traffic Act etc. By tradition it was regarded as the highest form of law because of the supremacy or sovereignty of Parliament. For an Act of Parliament to be valid there has to be the consent of the Queen, the Lords and the Commons.

Secondary or Delegated Legislation

This is made by a body or authority outside Parliament using powers conferred on them by a specific Act of Parliament, they cover complicated and technical areas which Parliament does not have time or knowledge to deal with. An Act of Parliament may delegate power to other bodies to make orders, regulations or rules SECONDARY or DELEGATED LEGISLATION

- secondary legislation is concerned with detailed changes to the law made under powers from an existing Act of Parliament
- made by bodies other than Parliament (e.g. the Government, Ministers, the Queen, local authorities)
- effective as soon as they are made

Examples of Secondary legislation

1.   Orders in Councils (enacted by the Privy Council)
2.   Statutory Instruments (issued by government ministers of the Queen)
3.   Byelaws (enacted by local authorities)

Case law

Common law or case law

These were created by judicial decisions in made in courts. Case law was developed through creation of precedents.

Custom

Criteria for the recognition of custom:

- It must have existed from 'time immemorial', that is, 1189;
- It must have existed continuously within that period;
- It must have been exercised peaceably and without opposition;
- It must have been felt to be obligatory;
- It must be capable of precise definition;
- It must have been consistent with other customs;
- It must be reasonable.

Books of authority

- As well as the case law that has built up over the centuries there have been very influential writers who have stated the law at various times. The courts were originally reluctant to admit these as authority, but this is becoming more and more prevalent in the practice of the courts, sources of authority are:
- Coke's Reports
- Blackstone's Commentaries
- Dicey

Breakdown of the UK Courts

The hierarchical structure of the English courts connotes the principle that the decision of a higher court is binding on a court below it. Thereby, laying the very basis of the doctrine of precedent, also referred to by its Latin name "stare decisis" or 'let the decision stand'. This doctrine is the very heart of the English legal system.

The Breakdown of the Courts in the UK fundamentally rests upon the common law system. The key idea of the common law legal system is that it should be applied consistently and could be used to predict what courts might decide in a particular case. This practice is known as "Stare Decisis (Let the Decision Stand)". "Stare Decisis" in operation sets the framework for the doctrine of precedents which in essence means that when a new problem of law comes to the courts to be determined, the judgment form a rule to be followed in all similar future cases, thus making law more predictable and standardised.

In this way, a hierarchy of court structure was developed and this structure constitutes the idea that judges in the lower courts must follow decisions made in the higher courts of the hierarchy.

Nonetheless, the Hierarchy of Courts in the UK is better explained with the diagrams overleaf. Moreover, there has been considerable significance in the fact that some courts must also follow their own previous decisions and are said to be bound by themselves. The Hierarchy of Courts can be considered as consisting of five (5) levels as indicated in Diagram II page 3.

The Hierarchy of Courts

Although concerns have been expressed about the extent to which the European Court of Justice, the European Court of Human Rights as indicated on Diagram I. page 2 and the Privy Council is relevant to the Breakdown of the Court Hierarchy in the UK. These Courts will be discussed briefly regarding their limitations and powers.

The European Court of Human Rights and Privy Council

Decisions of the European Court of Human Rights are not binding on UK domestic courts, however, they are persuasive and a UK court can choose to follow a decision if it considers it just to do so. Likewise, decisions from the Judicial Committee of the Privy Council are highly persuasive but not binding on English courts. It can be said that these courts are limited due to their non- binding nature.

Diagram I. Hierarchy of UK Courts

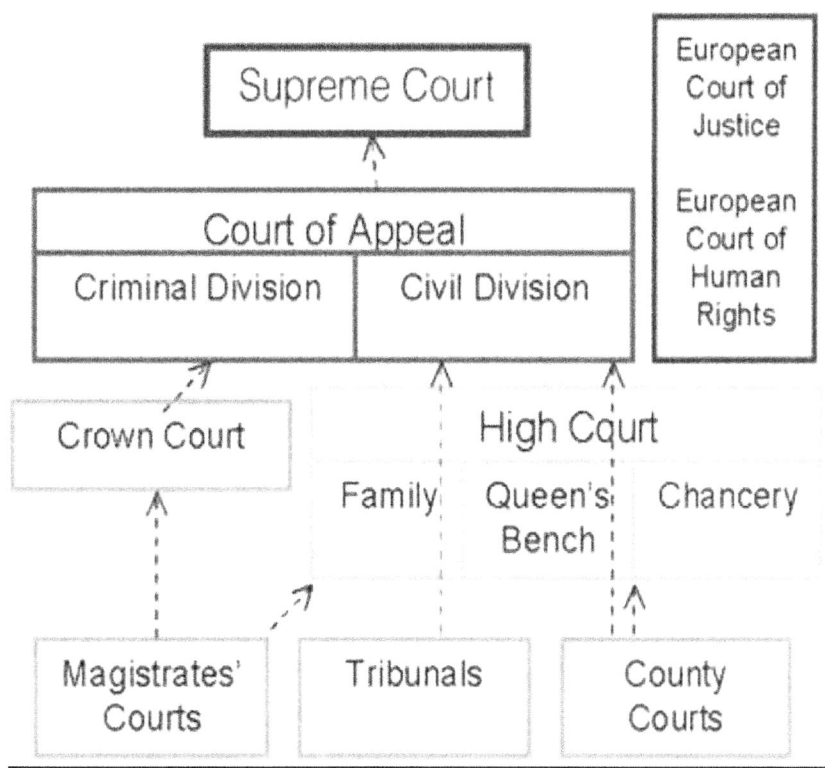

Courts in England

Diagram II. Hierarchy of UK Courts.

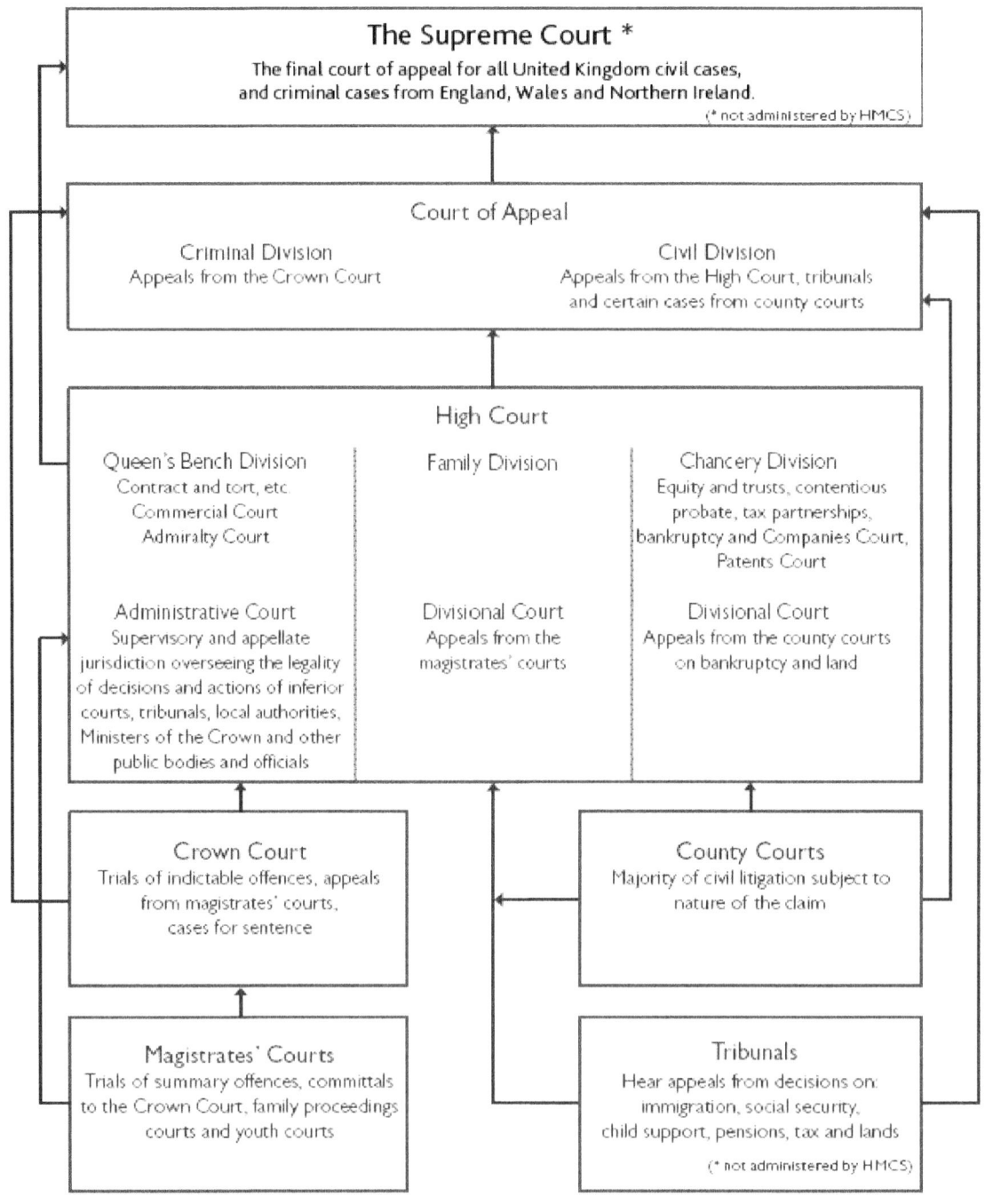

The Supreme Court and the European Court of Justice

(set to change of the exit of the UK from the EU early 2019). The Supreme Court is considered the highest decision making authority in England and Wales. In 2009 the Supreme Court replaced the House of Lords in England, Wales and Northern Ireland. At the top of the hierarchy is the Supreme Court, formally known as the House of Lords (Diagram I and II).

Decisions made in this court are binding on all other courts. However, up until 1966 it was bound by its own previous decisions, although this changed when the Lord Chancellor issued Practice Statement (Judicial Precedent) [1966] 1 WLR 1234 which stated the intention to depart from previous decisions when it appeared right to do so. Notwithstanding the fact that the Supreme Court is recognised as the highest English court, its powers are limited since the decisions made in the European Court of Justice bind all UK courts by virtue of sections 2 and 3 of the European Communities Act 1972.

The Court Of Appeal

The Court of Appeal is below the Supreme Court in the hierarchical structure and is split between the Civil and Criminal divisions. Decisions in both divisions bind lower courts and normally themselves but the Civil division is subject to exceptions to this rule as defined in the case of **Young v Bristol Aeroplane Co. Ltd (1944) (CA)**.

These proposed exceptions are:

- Where there is a conflict between two previous decisions. The court must decide which decision to follow and which to overrule.
- Where a previous decision has been overruled by the House of Lords (Supreme Court), the Court of Appeal must follow the decision of the superior court.
- Where its previous decision was made per incuriam meaning 'through carelessness' i.e. that a previous decision was made in

ignorance of some authority which would have led to a different conclusion.

A further exception than those cited above in **Young** is the effect of **s 3 of the European Communities Act 1972**. This could allow the Court of Appeal to ignore a previous decision that is inconsistent with EC law or later decision of the ECJ. However, in practice the Criminal division has more discretion in its obligation to follow precedent.

If it is apparent that a previous decision has been based on either a misunderstanding or misapplication of the law, a court in the criminal division is not bound to follow a previous decision.

The High Court

The Divisional Courts are located within the three division of the High Court, the jurisdiction of which is mainly appellate. They are bound by the doctrine of stare decisis following decisions from the Supreme Court and the Court of Appeal.

Divisional courts are above the High Court in the hierarchy and as such the decisions of these courts bind the ordinary cases of the High Court and also themselves with the exceptions in civil cases as cited in Young. In criminal appeal cases, the Queen's Bench divisional court may refuse to follow previous decisions if they are judged to have been made wrongly as in **R v Greater Manchester Coroner ex p Tal (1984) 3 ALL ER 240**.

The High Court is bound by decisions of those courts superior to it. Although decisions by individual high court judges have a strong persuasive authority on other high court judges, they are not binding on them. If two individuals' previous decisions are at variance, it is generally accepted that the latter decision should be followed, if the latter decision considered and provided grounds for not following the prior decision. This was established in **Colchester Estates v Carlton industries plc. (1984)**.

Crown Courts

Crown Courts are subject to binding precedent from superior courts but do not create precedents themselves and are not bound by their own previous decisions although their decisions are considered persuasive authority.

Magistrates and County Courts

Magistrates and County courts do not bind any other courts and are not bound by their own decisions.

Factually, it is not the decision that is the binding element but rather the legal reasoning for the decision based on the facts of the case. This is known as the ratio decidendi of a case or 'reason for deciding'. The ratio is the important part of a judgment as far as case law is concerned. This is the part that is binding on subsequent cases where the material facts are the same. Any part of the judgment that does not form part of the ratio is called obiter dictum or 'a statement by the way' and does not form part of the binding precedent.

The UK Police

The Police

The basic principles of Policing is that "crime is not a police problem, it is a community problem"

"Community Policing is a system-wide philosophy and management approach which promotes community, government and police partnerships to engage in pro-active problem solving to address causes of crime, fear of crime and other shared community issues."

The Police force in the UK is believed to be the brainchild of Sir Robert Peel in 1829 with the introduction of the Peelers or Bobbies (named after Robert Peel) were full-time paid uniformed police officers.

Their uniform and weaponry consisted of a hat, rattle, baton, and a blue uniform, the sought to prevention crime through foot patrols, it wasn't until 1884 that the Police whistle was introduced.

Sir Robert Peel was the home secretary who introduced in a series of Acts a central Police force; this took some time to establish but the Metropolitan Police Act in 1829 established Britain's first professional police force under the control of two police commissioners who were responsible directly to Robert Peel.

The force was initially established at 3,000 men, many recruited from existing Bow Street Runners and also from ex members of the army. Peel was an advocate for change and repealed the death penalty for larceny in shops and on board ships; in fact he gave the judges powers to refuse the death penalty for all crimes except murder, reducing the amount of executions immediately.

After Robert Peel became Prime Minister in 1835 the use of Gibbetting (or hanging dead bodies or body parts for public display) and Pillory (stocks) was abolished. Peel believed that there would be no reform in the criminal law until the Police were reformed and that crime rates would reduce when the Police lead by example not execution, the reform of the Police finally started when all counties in the Country were required to conform to a set of specific rules laid out in the County and Borough Police Act of 1856.

This led to the modern judicial system, criminology, a branch of sociology (why people do what they do) which has its modern roots in classicism and positivism, which began in the late 1800's. It took some 40 years for the death penalty to be removed by all judges and some continued to order the death penalty for menial crimes and the last recorded child to fall victim to the gallows was a nine year old boy from Essex who was found guilty of arson.

Sir Robert Peel's Nine Principles for Modern Policing

1. The basic mission for whom the police exist is to prevent crime and disorder.
2. The ability of the police to perform their duties is dependent upon public approval of police actions.
3. Police must secure the willing cooperation of the public in voluntary observance of the law to be able to secure and maintain the respect of the law.
4. The degree of cooperation of the public that can be secured diminishes proportionally to the necessity of the use of force.
5. Police seek and preserve public favour not by catered public opinion, but by constantly demonstrating absolute impartial service to the law.
6. Police use physical force to the extent necessary to secure observance of the law or to restore order only when exercise of persuasion, advice and warning is found to be insufficient.
7. Police at all times should maintain a relationship with the public that gives reality to the historic tradition; the Police are the public and the public are the police. The police being only those full time individuals charged with the duties that are incumbent on all citizens in the interest of community safety.
8. Police must secure the willing cooperation of the public in voluntary observance of the law to be able to secure and maintain the respect of the law.
9. The degree of cooperation of the public that can be secured diminishes proportionally to the necessity of the use of force.

The UK Police

One crucial role of the police is to oversee others in order to ensure that they keep to law and order in any society. This essentially means that the work of the police is to enforce public order and the law on a whole. However, individuals have the liberty to practice their individual rights, and in doing so they should not infringe on the rights others enjoy.

As such, the police's mandate to oversee the public's relationship is of a general nature. Thus, the role of serving the public became a paramount aspect to the functions of the police. The police became heavily involved in a wide array of activities that are meant to ensure a safe environment for the public and ultimately to prevent crimes and other infringement on individuals' rights. In this regard, important functions were integrated in the police service such as management, directing of traffic, directing tourists, attending to emergencies, and other functions beyond their normal scope of duties, with the main interest being to arrest law breakers and to enforce fines for offences.

Nonetheless, concerns were raised regarding the extent to which the police exercise their powers on individuals in the UK. Reference was made in particular to the high profile common law cases involving miscarriages of justice such as the Birmingham six and the Guilford four. This brought about questions related to the accountability of the police, the need for transparency in the methods used by the police and for the public's need of knowing their rights, if stopped or arrested by the police. The practice in connection with the exercising of various powers that is mandated to the Police Service correlates with "The Police and Criminal Evidence Act 1984". The aim of the Act is to amalgamate police powers under one code of practice and to carefully create equilibrium with respect to the rights of the individuals against the powers of the police.

Explanation of the Police and Criminal Evidence Act 1984 (PACE)

The Police and Criminal Evidence Act 1984 (PACE) is an important piece of legislation. It commenced January 01, 1986. Alongside its codes of practice, it provides the foundation and structure for policing powers and secures these policing powers around stop and search, arrest, detention, investigation, identification and interviewing detainees.

This provision repealed previous unsatisfactory and ambiguous statutory provisions on "stop and search". PACE, has created the right balance between the powers of the police and the rights and freedoms of the public and this balance is fundamental in order for PACE to work.

Stop and Search Powers

"Stop and Search" Powers are contained in Section 1 of PACE which states in part that a constable may search a person or vehicle in public for stolen or prohibited articles (defined as offensive weapons, articles used for the purpose of burglary or related crimes and professional display fireworks).

Under **section 1(1) (a) and (b) Police and Criminal Evidence Act 1984,** A police officer can use their power to stop and search in any place the public has ready access to or by implied permission have access (but not a dwelling). Private land is excluded if the person stopped is a non-resident or trespasser section 1 (4) (a) (b) Pace.

Section 1 (2) Police and Criminal Evidence Act 1984 states that an officer subject to subsections (3) and (5) can detain a person or vehicle for the purposes of a search. Anything which is in or on the vehicle can also be subject to a search.

Section 1 (3) Police and Criminal Evidence Act 1984 states the officer has no right to search any person/vehicle unless they have "Reasonable Suspicion" that prohibited/stolen articles will be found.

Reasonable suspicion should not come from generalisations or stereotypical images of certain groups. Religion should never be used as a reason to stop someone for the purposes of a search. The Race Relations Act 2000 makes it unlawful for police officers to discriminate on the grounds of race, colour, ethnic origin, nationality or national origins when using their powers. Stops should be made as a result of intelligence or by the officer witnessing suspicious behaviour enough to warrant a stop to search.

If an item is recovered during the search which the officer suspects to be a prohibited/stolen article the officer may seize that item. S1 (7) Pace sets out what prohibited articles are. They include:-

- Stolen goods
- Offensive weapons including bladed or sharply pointed items (excluding pocket knives with a bladed cutting edge not exceeding 3 inches).
- Articles intended for use in certain theft act offences
- Articles intended for destroying or damaging property added by s1 Criminal Justice Act 2003 e.g. Spray paint cans and tools to cause graffiti
- Fireworks within the definition of fireworks in s1 Fireworks Act 2003

Other stop and search powers allow the police to search for other items such as:-

- Drugs (Misuse of Drugs Act)
- Alcohol at sporting events, Sporting events (Control of Alcohol) Act 1985
- Contraband, Customs and Excise management Act 1979
- Firearms and crossbows, Firearms Act

When an officer detains a person for a stop a record of that stop has to be made. *S2 Police and Criminal Evidence Act 1984* provide statutory safeguards in relation to Police and Criminal Evidence Act 1984 and any other stop and search power. Before searching a person or vehicle or detain a person for the purposes of a search, the officer must take reasonable steps to bring to the persons attention as set out in s2 (3) (a) (b) (c) Pace:-

- His/her name
- The police station he/she is attached to
- The object of the search
- His grounds for making the search

The officer should also advise the person they are entitled to a written record of the search, and which police station they should apply to obtain the information (Para 2.6 code A) The police use the acronym GOWISE-LY to remind officers of each requirement of the search

G - Grounds for the search

O - Object of the search

W - Warrant card (if in plain clothes)

I - Identify. The officer must identify themselves

S - Station where the officer works

E - Entitlement to a copy of the search

L - Legal power being used for the detention

Y- "You are being detained for the purposes of a search..." The person must be informed they are being detained.

In *Osman V DPP 1999 EWHC Admin 622* the officers had not identified themselves or their station to the suspect making the search unlawful. S3 (1) Police and Criminal Evidence Act 1984 states, that when an officer conducts a search, they must make a written record of the search unless it is not practical to do so. If it is not practical to do so a written record must be made as soon as is reasonably possible after the completion of the search. When a police officer conducts a search in public only the outer coat/jacket and gloves can be searched. A more detailed search can be made in a police van out of public view but it must be conducted by an officer of the same sex.

Currently modern policing now actually covers a diverse range of jobs. Hence, specialist departments and units were created within the police.

The Different Departments in the Police Service

Criminal Investigations Department (CID)

CIDs deals with investigations into serious crimes. These count as robberies, burglaries, sexual offences, fraud, serious assaults and murders. CID officer sometimes assist uniformed officers in investigating the less serious crimes, such as theft. The CID has the same rank structure as the uniformed branch. Officers are known as detective constable, detective sergeants and so on.

A major inquiry can demand of CID officers working every hour of the day. The work is often slow and requires great patience as well as good memory and attention to detail

SOCA

SOCA or the Serious Organised Crime Agency was created in April 2006, the Agency having been formed from the amalgamation of the National Crime Squad (NCS), National Criminal Intelligence Service (NCIS), that part of HM Revenue and Customs (HMRC) dealing with drug trafficking and associated economic crime and the part of UK Immigration dealing with organised immigration crime (UKIS).

Their stated aim is to prevent and detect serious organised crime and to contribute to its reduction in other ways. In addition, SOCA is tasked to provide support to law enforcement partners, notably UK police forces and HM Revenue and Customs. Their work often involves very extensive and time consuming operations. Operations include undercover work, physical or technical surveillance, witness protection and financial investigation.

It effectively replaced the National Crime Squad with a remit to tackle all forms of organised crime. It comprises four functions – investigation, enforcement, intervention and corporate services... SOCA's main activities are fighting drugs trafficking, organised immigration crime, individual and private sector fraud – almost any crime where there is an organised element.

Drugs squad

Where the SOCA tackles the large-scale drug trafficking, local forces have squads to deal with drug offences in their area. They will be involved in surveillance of local drug dealers, raids on premises and making arrests and will often work closely with their national counterparts.

Economic Crime Unit/Detective

Established in 1946 and run by the Metropolitan Police in cooperation with the City of London Police, this unit also operates within the Serious Fraud Office. The SFO is a government department established to investigate large-scale fraud. Some regional forces also have specialist units dealing primarily with fraud.

Specialist Operations

Specialist Operations has branches covering a wide range of functions, including:

- Anti-terrorism
- Covert operations & intelligence
- Diplomatic protection
- Firearms
- National identification
- Photographic and graphics
- Royal protection
- Special Branch

Police Departments

Special Branch

Each force has its own Special Branch dealing with terrorism. Its work covers investigations into firearms or explosives, which may be linked with threats to national security. This involves surveillance work and also keeping regular officers informed of any threats. Established over a century ago to tackle the threat posed by the Irish nationalists who took to terrorism tactics, its post-war remit expanded to other perceived threats to national security.

Firearms Branch

Each Force has a number of officers in a specialist team who are trained and equipped to participate in operations that require firearms. Extremely thorough training is part of becoming a specialist firearms officer, while qualities of calmness and quick thinking are essential.

Traffic department

A traffic officer is concerned with all aspects of road safety, while still getting involved in policing all kinds of non-traffic incidents. The duties of traffic officers are included below:

- dealing with motorway pile-ups and road accidents
- checking that vehicles on the road conform to the legal safety requirements
- dealing with motoring offences, such as speeding
- breath testing procedures and dealing with drink driving offences
- managing the traffic when the road is blocked by an incident or accident
- court proceedings to support a prosecution

Drivers of traffic cars (and motorcycles) operate independently and are based in special premises.

Police Departments

Royal and diplomatic branch

Police in this branch are responsible for the protection of members of the royal family and their residences, and also embassies and diplomats. They are highly trained in the use of firearms, self-defence and advanced driving skills.

Dog handlers

Dog Handling Teams harness the powers of dogs' senses of smell and hearing to assist with the detection and prevention of crime. Dog handlers are also used by many agencies outside of the police including HM Revenue and Customs, the armed forces, fire and rescue services and prison services. The role of a police dog handler is to assist the police in a wide range of specialist roles including:

- Search for explosives, weapons and narcotics
- Aid in the search for missing or injured people
- Track and detain offenders who are on the run from the police
- Locating dead bodies and blood, either buried or on the surface
- Airport and port control

Mounted Police

Horses are mainly used by the police for:

- crowd control during demonstrations and sporting events
- imposing a police presence in serious disturbances such as riots (horses are trained to remain calm even under the noisiest and most violent conditions)
- in rural areas, horses are used in searches of wide open spaces
- in London, the Metropolitan Police horses take part in ceremonial occasions and are ridden on patrol

River police

Forces with large rivers or coastal waters within their area will have a river police section to assist in the policing the following situations:

- assisting boats in difficulties
- inspecting docks, riverside premises and landing places
- dealing with thefts from ships, houseboats and riverside warehouses
- rescuing people (sometimes retrieving bodies) from the water
- making safe drifting boats, or other objects which can cause hazards on the water
- monitoring water pollution
- working with HM Revenue and Customs to counter smuggling
- searching for suspects and criminals

Underwater Search Unit

Highly trained divers are needed in many forces to take part in underwater search units. The units are called in for underwater searches for suspected weapons, stolen property or missing people.

The Prison service HMS Prisons

Prisons are generally referred to as correctional institutions and have been a central part of the Criminal Justice System in the UK.

When a legal penalty is imposed, offenders found guilty are normally sent to prison. However, the Prison is well thought-out to be the last resort, unless the circumstances surrounding the offence warrant a prison sentence.

In the past, prisons have been a controversial subject matter and recent developments have suggested that members of the public condemns the prison as a result of the recent developments related to whether prisons are effective or whether they are ineffective in rehabilitating criminals into law-abiding citizens.

Prisons were established to detain convicted offenders who have been certified and designated there by judges. Within the United Kingdom, there are two levels of prisons, namely, the Federal Level and Provincial/Territorial Level. Thus, people who serve two years or less are designated at provincial or territorial prisons, while inmates who serve more than two years are designated at federal prisons.

Over the years, prisons have gone through fundamental changes. Punishment in relation to being sentenced to a prison term has become very essential for certain types of law that is broken. Nonetheless, there have been issues with the prison recently. Academic Scholars such as Criminologists, Sociologists and various scholars have debated both in favour of the success on one hand and failures of the prison on the other hand.

Hence, the presumption that the prison does not rehabilitate offenders, but instead makes them bad was suggested. Other scholarly argument is that prisons are really effective and they are an indispensable institution in the criminal justice system since the prison helps to improve at some point all those who have committed crimes.

History of the Prison Service

The most commonly known and traceable history related to justice for crimes and wrongdoing was in the medieval period where they mainly drowned criminals. Nonetheless, by the 10th century the British changed their justice to another relatively barbaric practice, through the prolific use of hanging.

This was a time where people were hanged for crimes as minor as bogging and petty theft. This sanction was not partial to anyone, as small children caught stealing food to survive were publically hanged, old people, pregnant women, and the mentally impaired etc. were all hanged for small crimes.

A different approach was taken in the 1300s to accommodate all populations of criminals in prisons together. Although Prisons became popular on this note they became very unsanitary, overcrowded, dangerous, and totally inhumane from even the most puritan standpoint. Due to the appalling conditions prisoners paid guards to unlock, feed, unchain and finally, release them.

The obvious setback was that the upper classes were seldom found in such places, and the pitiful poor were all too frequently sent there. Interestingly this initial concept of the prisoner paying their way through their sentence still appears in the service today. However, guards in that era were not employed by the state, but in the literal sense, by the prisoners.

A forward approach also, took place in the late 1700s. There emerged prison ships and later the deportation of convicts to the New World. This was due to the overcrowding in prisons and the fact public executions were still the most preferential type of justice. As a result of this, Australia was populated by many of those who were deemed to be criminal, America had their fair share with those repatriated in to the British army and many other far flung countries of the time were bestowed with those who had the choice of deportation or death.

Moreover, the late 1700s brought about a humanitarian move toward corrections through John Howard and his Quaker peers.

Another interesting point was the historical context with regard to the revolution in France which gave an open warning to the monarchy at the time that the proletariat would and could overthrow the crown should they so desire and should their mistreatment from the state continued. Moving on, the 1800s saw the emergence of Jailers who were paid for their services by the state, thus alleviating mistreatment of prisoners to the extent that was previously apparent.

In addition, the 20th Century saw the prison system in England has directly affected by the political parties that were in power at the time. The Conservatives were known for their tough approach to law and order and had a greater amount of incarceration be carried whenever they were in government, thus being known as the party of law in order. However, the 1970s seen the Labour party taking control and a different approach to incarceration was adopted. A greater focus on the rehabilitation of offenders was adopted under labour moving away from the concept of incarceration and a direct move towards programs that could be seen to be of use in the rehabilitation of offenders was embraced.

Interestingly though, even though these concentrations on the empowerment of offenders to make choices not to offend, by addressing substance abuse, offending behaviour, anger management and the like, there was still a high amount of incarceration and further to this recidivism. There are numerous ideas regarding the lack of efficacy within these approaches, ranging from a lack in adequate funding, follow through of services and a booming population in the UK.

Probation Department

Probation

Probation is a type of punishment that permits 'criminals' to be released into society on detailed conditions for example the condition that they keep in contact with their probation officer, this could include home visits and inform probation officers of any changes to living conditions, i.e. change of address.

The Criminal Justice Act 1991 facilitated and secured the rehabilitation of criminals and also protects the public from serious harm. This gave courts the broad-spectrum to combine punishment with a financial penalty. This essentially doubled the effect of their action which in actuality works as another deterrence effect, if potential offenders and offenders alike are made aware that even what the public view as petty crimes such as graffiti and the like have strong consequences.

As Feely and Simons (1992) indicated that probation 'is a form of low-cost surveillance for low-risk offenders", probation however, has various points of view and this depends on the crime committed.

Role and Function of the Probation Service

The role of the Probation Service is to decrease prisoners and to help deter petty criminals and those who intend to commit crimes. A probation order brings the offender into the public view and mainly functions to protect both the offender and public.

Although, major areas of the probation service and the way it is structured and governed have been altered over the years, the prevention of offenders reoffending has always been at the forefront of its work.

The Probation of Offenders Act 1907 initially provided the statutory foundation of the probation service and made it possible for Magistrates' Courts to appoint probation officers who were paid by the local authority. The Act upheld the idea that probation officers are there to 'advise, assist and befriend' those under supervision. .

Further, the Criminal Justice Act 2003 later furnished the Probation Service with an updated statutory framework to address the ever changing body. The Act connotes that the purpose of sentencing was to: punish offenders; for crime reduction; for the reform and rehabilitation of offenders; for the protection of the public; and the making of reparation by offenders to persons affected by their crimes.

Nevertheless, on a practical ideal, probation personnel has emphasized that the original values of probation is:

1. the particular belief in the possibility of personal change,
2. scepticism about the value of prison as the way to reduce crime,
3. respect for diversity and the importance of professional relationships in enabling change.

Due to these identified ideals, the role of probation officers has been given a significant transformation from exclusively providing a service to offenders in the community through the courts to providing through-care (in prison) and after-care (post-release supervision) to those who have received custodial sentences.

At one time, magistrates' courts in particular expected what would today be regarded as a high level of staff to advise the Bench and provide reports. Napo, the trade union and professional association for family court and probation staff, emphasised that probation work starts in court: "The probation service provides impartial, accurate, reliable, skilled and professional advice to assist the courts in making their decisions".

 Some of the works probation officers provide are pre-sentence reports such as oral, fast delivery and standard delivery reports. These reports vary by the depth and detail of the assessment carried out and due to the amount of time required for preparation and the court's assistance in determining the most suitable method of dealing with an offender. The Magistrates' Association maintains that the post-court role and function of probation staff is to: coordinate a sentence; monitor progress; ensure compliance; and monitor and report breaches. Accredited programmes for offenders were originated in the late 1990s. The premise upon which these programmes were designed was by the use of research on how best to influence people's attitudes and thinking. These programmes were seen as the main type of intervention to reduce re-offending and have demonstrated its effectiveness.

Some programmes are generic (i.e. suitable for most offenders), while others were designed for particular types of offence (for example, sex offending or violence) or offender (e.g. Women's Acquisitive Crime Programme.

Magistrates' and County Courts

These are called the inferior or lower courts. They are bound by the High Court, Court of Appeal and House of Lords. Decisions in the Magistrates Court are not reported, their precedents cannot be binding, or even persuasive ones; like the Crown Court, they are not bound by their own decisions. Magistrates' courts are presided over by Justices of the Peace (magistrates). Cases are normally heard before a bench of two or three Justices of the Peace, this power is conveyed by Section.121 ***Magistrates' Court Act 1980.*** Justices of the Peace do not need to be legally qualified, they may be given advice about matters of law by a justices' clerk.

Civil Jurisdiction of Magistrates Court

Civil cases are predominately licensing, family proceedings, and the care and adoption of children. Certain civil debts, for example in relation to income tax, may be recovered in a magistrates' court.

The Crown Court

The Crown Court is bound by all the courts above it. Its decisions do not form binding precedents, though when High Court judges sit in the Crown Court, their judgments form persuasive precedents, which must be given serious consideration in successive cases, though it is not obligatory to follow them.

The main jurisdiction of the Crown Court is to that of trial on indictment, before judge and jury, Section.46 Senior Courts Act 1981. Following the Criminal Justice Act 2003, it is possible for thinking point

Trial in the Crown Court is more time- consuming and costly than trial in the magistrates' courts. The classification of offences determines where a trial may take place. By reclassifying offences as summary, trial costs may be saved. Is such an approach defensible?

Sentencing

The Crown Court deals with cases that have been dealt with by the magistrates' court for sentence where the magistrates' court is of the opinion that its sentencing powers are inadequate.

Appeals in the Crown Court

There are several appeal routes from the Magistrates Court to Crown Court, including:

- against sentence where a defendant pleads guilty;
- against sentence or conviction where a defendant pleads not guilty; and against licensing decisions.

County Court

Circuit judges carry out the majority of county court work, one or more of who is assigned to each county court district, and by district judges and deputy district judges. Jurisdiction is given to the county court by Section 5 ss. 8, ss 8 County Courts Act 1984. These courts are civil and governed by the County Courts Act 1984.

The jurisdiction of the county courts includes the following:

- contract or tort cases under **Section.15 County Courts Act 1984;**
- provided the High Court has not been given exclusive jurisdiction, a county court may hear and make an order for the recovery of money under, **Section 16 County Courts Act 1984;**
- actions where title in land is in question, **Section 21 County Courts Act1984;**
- equity jurisdiction, subject to a £30,000 limit; and
- probate, subject to a £30,000 limit.

Jurisdiction is also conferred on the county courts by other statutes, for example:

Country court is also a divorce court and shall have jurisdiction to hear and determine any matrimonial case, these are started in the county court and proceed to the high court.

Commencing proceedings – county courts or High Court

In civil cases, the two courts of trial are the county courts and the High Court.

County court or high court is determined by the amount of the claim

- a case cannot commence in the High Court unless the value of the claim is more than £25,000; and
- if a case concerns personal injuries it must not commence in the High Court unless the claim is worth £50,000 or more.

Small claims jurisdiction

Claims of less than £5,000 are allocated to the faster small claims track. The procedure involved should allow litigants to appear without legal representation. The hearing is to be informal and the court may adopt a proceeding that it considers to be fair; the strict rules of evidence do not apply. The apparent advantages are that the small claims procedure is

- quicker, less costly and stressful, and is flexible. Nevertheless, litigants should consider alternatives
- to going to court such as seeking to negotiate or agreeing to seek mediation. Note
- that the suggestion that a claimant should consider alternative ways of resolving a dispute,

Appeals in the County Court

There is a limited appellate jurisdiction whereby circuit judges may hear appeals from the decisions of district judges.

High Court

High Court judges, alternatively known as puisne (junior) judges, sit in the High Court.

The High Court is mainly a civil court. It is comprised of three divisions: the Queen's Bench Division; the Chancery Division; and the Family Division, **Section.5 Senior Courts Act 1981.**

Appellate jurisdiction

The High Court also acts as a court of appeal in certain instances. A major appellate function in criminal cases is exercised by the Queen's Bench Division. Appeals are heard following summary trial before a magistrates' court by way of case stated where it is alleged that the decision is wrong in law or was given in excess of jurisdiction,

Section.111 Magistrates' Courts Act 1980 also, an appeal from a magistrates' court to the Crown Court following summary trial may be further appealed, by defence or prosecution, by way of case stated to the Divisional Court of the Queen's Bench Division, s.28 Senior Courts Act 1981. The grounds once again are that the decision is wrong in law or is in excess of jurisdiction.

Court of Appeal

Judges in the Court of Appeal are termed Lords Justices of Appeal (also known as LJ) The Court of Appeal (Civil Division) is wholly appellate. Appeals from the county courts and the High Court are governed by Civil Procedure Rules,

Supreme Court

The first Justices of the Supreme Court were the 'law lords' or Lords of Appeal in Ordinary from the House of Lords. They still carry their title of Lord or Lady. However, new appointments are not made Life Peers but are to be given the courtesy title of Lord or Lady; The court consists of twelve justices and they usually sits in panels of five but may also sit in panels of seven or nine. The panels of seven or nine are constituted when a previous decision is asked to be, or may be, departed from, the case raises an issue of constitutional significance, or the issue raised is one of great public importance.

The jurisdiction of the Supreme Court is as the ultimate court of appeal in the United Kingdom, hearing both civil and criminal appeals, together with the devolution jurisdiction of the Privy.

Chapter Six – Prisons in the UK

Penology in the UK

The early penal system

The was little need for prisons in the UK prior to the 1600s, due mainly in part to most offences carrying the death penalty and the innocent were set free, except for soldiers, soldiers were held in dungeons, there was a number of dungeons throughout the country which held prisoners of war.

However as the century passed there was clearly a need for an alternative to the death penalty for even the merest of offences like stealing bread etc. It was in 1615 that Thomas More wrote made the suggestion in his reform proposal called Utopia that those who were convicted of stealing be imprisoned rather that executed and also released as slaves upon sentencing finishing.

There were however some prisons in the later 1600s, these were debtors prisons, which was contradictory in nature as prisons in this era were akin to lodging houses, the prisoners had to pay for their keep, if they did not they were thrown into county jails were was no fate for anyone due to poor sanitation and disease, few made it out alive, even for the smallest of debts.

Transportation

Transportation became an alternative to the expensive incarceration, prisoners who avoided the noose were shipped out to colonies and plantation in the British colonies such as Jamaica and Barbados, after the War of Independence this all changed and ships were then sent to the new land in Australia where there designated colonial prisons, people were sent to Australia on hulk ships, these ships took those who were found guilty but not hanged to serve their sentences in the penal colonies.

Prisons in the UK

The first state prison was opened in the UK in 1779 it was in London, and called Milbank, however this was closed in the early 1800s due to poor sanitation and the large death tolls from illness of the inmates.

In 1877 prisons became State-run services and HMP Wormwood Scrubs was built, the first warden was called Du Cane, Du Cane was a strict man and was an advocate of bread and water, solitary labour and religious instruction.

The Modern Prison Service

The introduction into law of the Criminal Justice Act 1991 changed the prison services in the UK, all prisoners were given internal sanitation in their cells and the old slop out was banned, all new constructed prisons in the UK after this introduction had to have toilets in the cells. However showers were not and still have not been made compulsory in the cells.

There are currently 150 active prisons in the UK, with an average daily population of 85,981 consisting of 82,086 males and 3,895 females52.

Her Majesty's Inspectorate of Prisons (HMIP's) mandate is set out in the Prison Act 1952 as amended by the Criminal Justice Act 1982, the Immigration and Asylum Act 1999, the Immigration, Asylum and Nationality Act 2006 and the Police and Justice Act 2006.

Her Majesty's Inspectorate of Prisons

HMIP is responsible for inspecting all prisons in England and Wales, including young offender institutions; all removal centres, short-term holding facilities and escort arrangements for immigration detainees; and all police custody facilities.

The Prisons and Probation Ombudsman

The PPO's duty includes the following: to investigate all deaths in prisons or probation hostels— whether they occur from natural causes, homicide or are self-inflicted.

This is to give effect to Article 2 of the ECHR (European Convention on Human Rights); this is legislation which states that the State has a procedural duty to investigate deaths in circumstances where it has acquired a positive duty of care to protect life.

Chapter Seven – Prisons & Policing in Ireland

Penology in Ireland

The Early Penal System in Ireland

The early penal system in Ireland really only took shape after the introduction of incarceration, before the 18th century goals (prisons where those on remand were kept) were a dumping ground for debtors and vagrants. The Irish Prisons Act of 1826 saw the introduction of Bridewells, until then there were few reform institutions as punishment was usually capital or severe enough to deter future criminal behaviour.

Cesare Baccaria's article on crime and punishment was published in 1864 after this the Irish Penal System started to improve slowly, there was the introduction of Bride wells (petty offender prisons), this happened when the prison reformer John Howard made a trip to Ireland, here he noted the corruption in the Irish Prison Service.

A plethora of prisons or goals were built in the 19th century and many were designed and built to Jeremy Bentham's design. This was a circular guards hall with arms surrounding, this mean that guards could see all prisoners at all times. Mountjoy was built on this design. Kilmainham goal was built in 1789 and closed in 1910, this prison held many of the rebels from the 1916 Easter rising which saw them executed in the disused prison in May 1916. These prisons saw a great increase in times of Marshall law such as 1798 and 1804 and such times as there was outbreaks and ward of Independence.

Prisons were normally places where people were sent to reform, to retribution and punishment, however the 19th century saw a new prison,

Grangegorman, this was a woman's prison, it was not based on punishment, it was based on moral reforming, unlike modern prisons there was segregation of prisoners, those who were convicted of minor or petty offences and those convicted of major offences, the authorities were careful not to allow the petty interact with the major criminals, this was to stop the petty thieves being influenced by the major criminals, it was used in the late 19th Century when prisoners were sent there while awaiting deportation.

Prisons in Ireland held prisoners from all walks of life and sentences for theft, prostitution, drunk and disorderly behaviour and vagrancy were the most common, even offences life swearing warranted a prison sentence for some.

Penology in Ireland

Ireland saw an huge increase in the prison population in the mid 1800's this was due to the great famine, many people committed offences which would see them incarcerated, this was better than going hungry or even dying from hunger.

Many prisoners who committed petty crimes around this time were sent to Spike Island in Cork and then transported to Tasmania (of the coast of Australia) to serve their sentences; it was rare for any convict to return to Ireland after serving their transportation sentences.

The Modern Prison Service

Political responsibility for the Prison System in Ireland is vested in the Minister for Justice and Equality. The Irish Prison Service operates as an executive agency within the Department of Justice and Equality. It is headed by a Director General supported by 7 Directors. The Irish Prison Service is administered centrally with its headquarters located at IDA Business Park, Ballinalee Road, Longford, Co. Longford

The Prison Service operates within a statutory framework comprising:

1. the Prisons Acts, including the most recent Prisons Act 2007,
2. relevant provisions in other statutes such as the Prisons (Visiting Committees) Act, 1925, the Criminal Justice Act, 1960, the Criminal Justice (Miscellaneous Provisions) Act, 1997, the Criminal Justice Act, 2007, other criminal justice acts and the Transfer of Sentenced Persons Acts, 1995 and 1997 and
3. the Rules for the Government of Prisons, 2007.

For persons held on immigration related matters the main legislative provisions are the Immigration Acts 1999, 2003 and 2004, their associated regulations, the Illegal Immigrants Trafficking Act 2000 and the Refugee Act 1996.

The Prison Service also takes due account of the UN and European Conventions on Human Rights, UN Standard Minimum Rules for the Treatment of Prisoners, the UN Convention against Torture and other Cruel, Inhuman or Degrading Treatment or Punishment, the UN Covenant on Civil and Political Rights, the European Convention for the Prevention of Torture and Inhuman or Degrading Treatment or Punishment.

Ireland's Prisons

Location of Prisons and Places of Detention

Ireland's Prisons

There are 14 institutions in the Irish Prison System consisting of 11 traditional "closed" institutions, two open centres which operate with minimal internal and perimeter security, and one "semi-open" facility with traditional perimeter security but minimal internal security (the Training Unit). The majority of female prisoners are accommodated in the purpose-built "Dóchas Centre" and the remainder are located in a separate part of Limerick Prison.

Mountjoy: Committal prison for adult male prisoners, at North Circular Road, Dublin 7.

Dóchas: Committal prison for female prisoners aged

17 years and over at North Circular Road, Dublin 7

Limerick: Committal prison for adult male and female, at Mulgrave Street, Limerick.

Cork: Committal prison for adult male prisoners, at Rathmore Road, Cork.

Castlerea: Committal prison for adult male prisoners, at Harristown, Castlerea, Co. Roscommon.

Cloverhill: Committal prison for remand adult male prisoners, at Cloverhill Road, Clondalkin, Dublin 22

Arbour Hill: Prison for adult male prisoners, at Arbour Hill, Dublin 7.

Midlands: Prison for adult male prisoners, at Dublin Road, Portlaoise, Co. Laois.

Portlaoise: Prison for adult male prisoners, including the detention of high security prisoners, at Dublin Road, Portlaoise, Co. Laois

Wheatfield : Prison for adult male prisoners, at Cloverhill Road, Clondalkin.

Shelton Abbey: An open centre for male prisoners aged 19 years and over, Arklow, Co. Wicklow

St. Patricks Institution: An institution for male juveniles aged 16 to 21 years, at North Circular Road, Dublin 7.

Loughan House: An open centre for the detention of male prisoners aged 18 years and over, at Blacklion, Co. Cavan

Training Unit: A semi-open place of detention for male prisoners aged 18 years and over, at Glengarriff Parade, Dublin 7, for industrial training.

Probation Service and the Irish Criminal Justice System

The Role of the Probation Service within the Irish Criminal Justice System in Ireland

The Probation Service is an agency of the Department of Justice and Equality. The Probation Service is sometimes involved in the Criminal Justice Process between the prosecution and trial phase, for example, when a court requires a Probation Officer to hold a family conference. More often, the Probation Service become involved in the criminal justice process, between the trial and sanction phases, often in cases where a trial court requires a pre-sanction assessment and report to assist in deciding on an appropriate sanction. In some cases, the court may be considering placing an offender on probation supervision or community service.

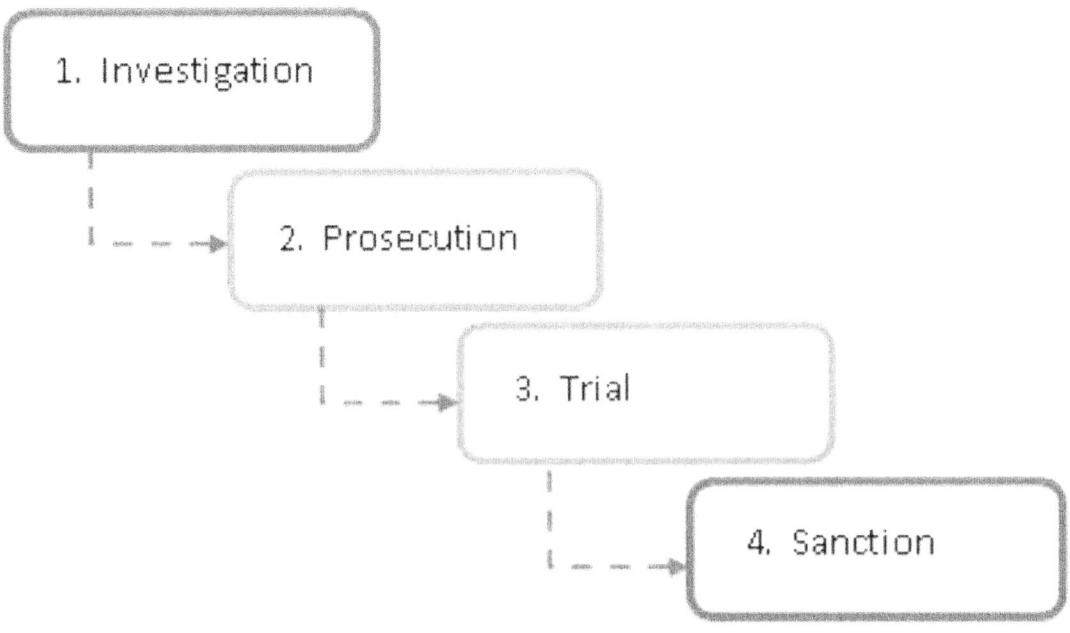

Where the court decides on a community-based sanction, the Probation Service is responsible for managing the sanction and supervising the offender. They help offenders to become better citizens and make good the harm done by crime. The Probation Service also undertakes whatever steps are appropriate to reduce the risk of future harm or re-offending by the offender.

47

---

[47] https://l00111551.wordpress.com/2014/02/19/crime-and-criminal-justice-in-ireland-week-3/

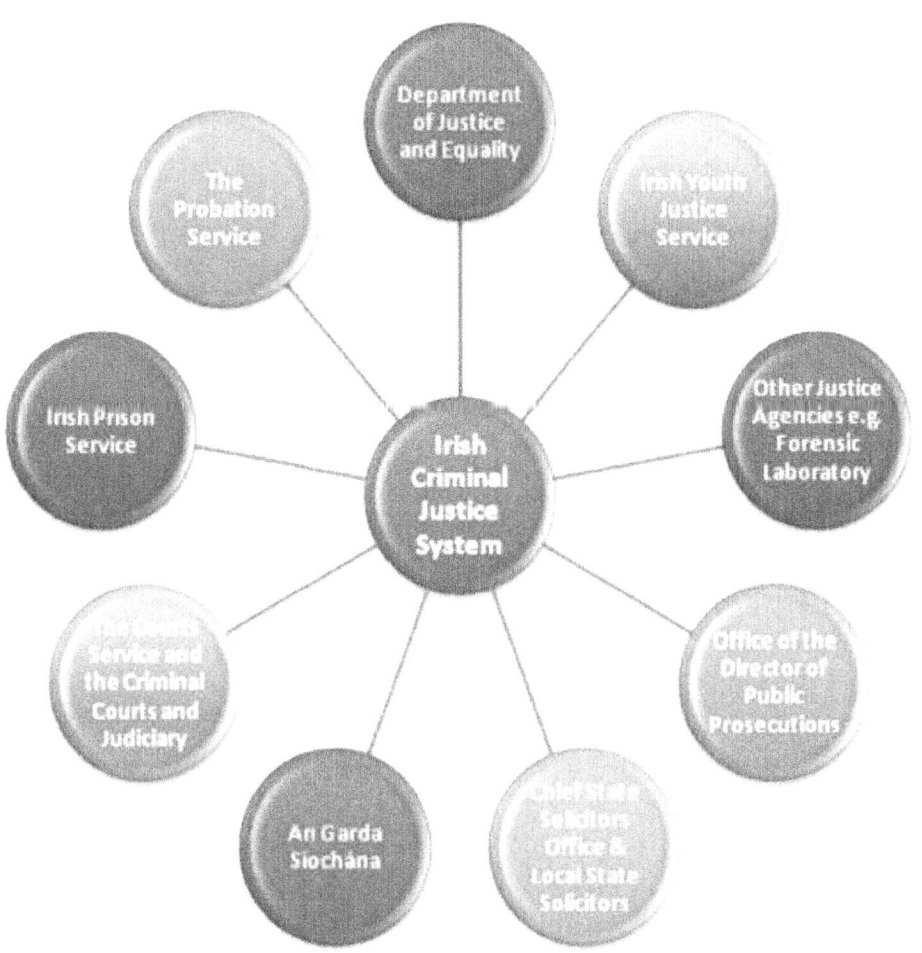

48

The Probation Service has an important role in planning and preparing for the release of prisoners and their return to the community. They also supervise some offenders after their release from prison. This particular role is focused on reintegrating the offender into society, with the priority of protecting the public and reducing the risk of re-offending.

The Probation Service works closely with the other agencies of the criminal justice system, as illustrated in the diagram below, to reduce crime and make communities safer.

---

[48] https://l00111551.wordpress.com/2014/02/19/crime-and-criminal-justice-in-ireland-week-3/

The Irish Police – The Gardaí

The Garda Siochána

History of the Gardaí

An Garda Síochána was formed in 1922, until this time policing was the job of the Royal Irish Constabulary (RIC) and Dublin Metropolitan Police.

After the signing of the Anglo Irish Treaty the new state would not allow the RIC to continue due to its British roots and loyalties, the Metro continued until 1925 when it was amalgamated with the Gardaí.

The Civic Guards

The push to recruit new Garda had at its heart new rules, members had to be single, over 5 feet 9 and be able to read write and pass maths. The first Commissioner of the new Garda force was Michael Staines. This first Garda were somewhat of a failure, while training in the military barracks in Kildare over 1000 new Gardaí broke ranks and stormed the armoury. This mutiny continued for over seven weeks and talks were exhaustive it was finally ended when Michael Collins took over the talks. Staines resigned amid claims that those opposed to the treaty were the main cause of the mutiny. By the end of 1922 the Guards were stationed throughout the Country, the transference was somewhat peaceful, however this peace was shattered when a barracks accident led to the death of a young Garda, it was after this time that arms were removed from the guards and they became arms free.

Criminal division of the Gardaí

It was on the same day as Michael Collins was shot on the 22nd August 1922 that the criminal division was established. This was separate to the civil guards and was formed from members of the Irish Republican Police and members of the Army. It consisted of over 100 heavily armed men and three women who posed as typists, but whose real job was to ferret out women engaged in anti-state activities.

By October 1923 the Free State was stable enough for the CID to be disbanded and its personnel transferred to the Dublin Metropolitan Police, by 1925 the DMP and CID were amalgamated with the Garda Síochána.

Modern Gardaí

The Mission of An Garda Síochána is: *Working with Communities to Protect and Serve.*

An Garda Siochana is a community based organisation with more than 15,000 Garda and civilian employees.

These include...

- Air Support Unit
- Ballistics Unit
- Mounted Unit
- Technical Support Services
- Water Unit
- National Bureau of Fraud Investigation
- Fingerprint Unit
- Photographic Unit National
- Drugs Unit
- Mapping Unit
- National Immigration Unit

There are other criminal divisions of the Gardai including:

Criminal Arrests

As defined in the **CRIMINAL JUSTICE ACT 1984 and CRIMINAL ASSETS BUREAU ACT 1996**

The Criminal Justice Act, 1984

Reinforced the powers of the Gardaí in their detention of suspects

- It also protected the rights of those suspects being detained in Garda custody. The first legislative power to detain a suspect was contained in **the Offences against the State Act 1939.**

Section 30 of The Criminal Justice Act of 1984 contained a statutory power to detain any suspect at a Garda station for questioning following their arrest, it authorises any member to detain a suspect following arrest for a period of 24 hours. A person may then be detained for a further period of 24 hours if such detention is authorised by a member not below the rank of Superintendent.

The power of detention in the Section 4 of The Criminal Justice Act of 1984 is normally invoked when detaining suspects at Garda stations for further questioning. Sections 4(1) and 4(2) states that the offence must be serious (indictable) , i.e. it must carry a possible sentence of over five years such as murder, assault causing harm, sexual offences, theft, etc. Sections 4(1) and 4(2) stated that there must be reasonable cause for the arrest and the detention must be necessary for a proper investigation of the offence.

These conditions must be satisfied in order for the arrest and detention to be lawful under Section 4 of the Criminal Justice Act of 1984.

If those rules are not adhered to, then a principle called the "Fruit of the poison tree": occurs, this means that if the arrest/detention is unlawful, any evidence arising from unlawfulness may not be used in the trial against the suspect.

The suspect's detention is timed from their arrest (not the time they arrive at the Garda station), this time starts of as six hours, again from the time of arrest, whereby the senior Garda must be advised of the nature of the crime, facts and evidence to date, any further enquiries needed, the Garda, not below Superintendent then decides if the suspect can be detained further. Between the hours of midnight to 8am the suspect can request the questioning be suspended and resumed at 8am. They are also entitled to rest periods, however they can waive those rights but this must be signed by the suspect.

Section 5 of The Criminal Justice Act of 1984; states that, a suspect is entitled to, access to a solicitor. Their next of kin must also be notified. If a suspect is denied any of these rights their conviction may be overturned. DPP V Healy

Section 6 of The Criminal Justice Act of 1984 deals with the powers available to the Gardaí in relation to someone in custody, such as taking their name, addresses, fingerprints etc. Gardaí have the powers to demand a suspect name, and address, search their person, take any swabs or fingerprints required and even skin samples, if the suspect is suspected of handling firearms or explosives. Finally, take and seize any property or possession of the suspect in relation to the investigation.

Section 7 of The Criminal Justice Act of 1984, this section was introduced to give effect to the Treatment of Persons in Custody Regulations.

They rules are set out on a sheet which is handed to the suspect on his arrival at the station, and he is asked to sign the custody record to indicate receipt of a copy of his rights, however by Subsection 3 of this Section states that non-occurrence of these right may not necessarily overturn the custody. As set out in Section 4, only a serious breach can overturn the custody.

Criminal Assets Bureau (CAB)

As defined in the ***CRIMINAL ASSETS BUREAU ACT 1996***

The Criminal Assets Bureau Act or CAB Act is believed to be one of the leading and advanced pieces of legislation to emerge from Ireland or the EU for that fact. This piece of legislation was enacted after the murder of Gerry McCabe and Veronica Guerin in 1996, by gangland criminals.

This legislation was introduced to curb the almost limitless power of gangland and drugs lords in Ireland, it means that whereby any proceeds of crime or proceeds from gangland or affiliation to them, drug dealers or criminals homes, bank accounts and private property could be seized, in essence the place where it hurt most. Until the enactment of this piece of legislation criminals could use the constitutional right to home and private property in their advantage and make it unconstitutional to take any of it, hence, allowing them to keep for themselves or their families the proceeds of their crimes.

Alongside the CAB Act the Bails Act 1997 was introduced, this piece of legislation allowed the courts to refuse bail if they were of the belief that an accused person would commit further offences while on bail. A far cry from the old Bail Act, which stated the accused, could be denied bail if there was a reasonable belief that they would interfere with a witness or not attend their hearing, this new, no longer was the presumption of innocence in the forefront, but in essence the presumption of guilt..!!

In its first ten years in operation, CAB collected €89 million in illegal assets.

As of 2016 it continues to be one of the most effective and dynamic pieces of legislation to deal with criminals and the proceeds of their crimes.

Special Detective Unit

The Special Detective Unit (SDU) is part of the Crime and Security branch and holds primary responsibility for State security.

The Irish Police – The Gardaí

Security and Intelligence Branch

The Security and Intelligence Branch was formed to counter the threat posed by domestic and international terrorist groups.

Domestic Violence Sexual Assault Investigation Unit

Domestic Violence Sexual Assault Investigation Unit is responsible for the Investigation of Sexual Crimes, Crimes against Children and Child Welfare. The Sex Offender Management and Intelligence Unit also works under this branch, it is responsible for maintaining a record of all persons who are subject to the requirements of the Sex Offenders Act 2001.

Along with the Air Support Teams, Community Policing and Mounted Units the Irish Gardaí is amongst the most progressive in the modern world and successful integration of community with a fair and just Policing of the Irish State.

The functions of the Gardaí

The Gardaí are responsible for making sure that the law of the State is obeyed and that those who do not obey the law are arrested and brought before the courts. Gardaí is the Irish word for "guardians". An Gardaí Siochana means "guardians of the peace". The primary function of An Garda Síochána is to ensure that people feel safe on the streets and in their homes. Building stronger and safer communities contributes greatly to improving the quality of life for the people.

The function of An Garda Síochána is to serve the community by implementing and upholding the law as legislated by Government. With the participation and dedication of the Gardaí, other community stakeholders (e.g. retail outlets, public services, public amenities) are, as far as possible, ensured of safety and they in turn commit to law abidance to serve the common good of the community. To ensure a positive strategy, issues such as the quality of the service provided and the strength and commitment of the partnerships amongst service providers and citizens must be ensured.

The Gardaí make a commitment to the community they serve, to provide:

- a good quality service,
- an open and transparent force which is accountable for its actions,
- the equal provision of services towards all members of the community who access the service or come into contact with the force,
- consultation and information to the local community on issues that impact them or may do so in the future and
- support to the local community activities by playing an active role.

Irish Courts System

The Court System in Ireland

The Petty Sessions

These were the courts of the lands, these courts dealt with both civil and criminal cases, however they are nothing like our modern courts, these courts in summary offences (relatively minor) had no judge, just a Justice of the Peace, this JoP was not legally qualified, usually a prominent member of the community whose decisions were final.

However, if there were serious or indictable (needing a jury) there were held four times per year, these were called quarterly sessions, and presided over by a Judge and jury. More serious offences were dealt with at assizes (hearings) on twice yearly basis, these were a two tier case, there were two juries, one (the grand) would hear if there was a case on legal fact, and the other trial jury which would decide the offenders guilt or innocence. Prisoners who were arrested between assizes were held on remand in goals such as Kilmainham and Grangegorman.

Superior Courts in Ireland (pre 1900)

Pre 1900 Ireland had several superior courts, the oldest and most significant were the Courts of Chancery, King's or Queen's Bench, Common Pleas and Exchequer which was renamed the Four Courts in 1877. These courts dealt predominately with administrative cases but it also dealt with legal matters. A Clerk of the Crown and Peace in each county maintained the records for each court.

The transition from the assizes to the modern system took place from 1900 to 1920; this was changed in 1920s with the introduction of the Dáil courts and the ordinary court system. This system was fraught with difficulty. The District Court replaced the Petty Sessions; the new Circuit Court was held in four districts and replaced the County courts, this system stayed until the introduction of the modern Court System.

Irish Courts System

The Supreme Court and court of Criminal Appeal

Both of these courts were established in 1924 under the Courts of Justice Act, 1924, which was given its powers by the Irish Free State (Constitution) Act, 1922, which was on foot of the Anglo Irish Treaty in 1921.53

Irish Courts System

The Function of the Courts

The courts system in Ireland has its historic origins in the British Courts System that was in use in Ireland up to 1922. The 1922 Constitution was enacted on the foundation of the Irish Free State. That Constitution provided for the setting up of new courts to replace the existing Courts that had evolved under the British administration. The Courts of Justice Act, 1924 established the legal basis for a new Court system.

Ireland has a written Constitution and Articles 34 to 37 of the Constitution deal with the administration of justice in general. Article 34.1 states that 'Justice shall be administered in Courts established by law'.

The Constitution outlines the structure of the court system as comprising:

- A court of final appeal, known as the Supreme Court,
- Courts of first instance which include the High Court with full jurisdiction in all criminal and civil matters and
- Courts of limited jurisdiction including
- the Circuit Court and the
- District Court organised on a regional basis.

The present courts were set up by the Courts (Establishment and Constitution) Act 1961 pursuant to Article 34 of the Constitution adopted by the Irish people in 1937. We are concerned mainly with the courts as they are relevant to personal injury and property litigation and we have focused on this area in the linked pages attached.

The Courts Act 2004 contains much that is relevant to the day-to-day handling of Personal Injury Claims within the Courts System.

- District Court
- Circuit Court

- High Court
- Central Criminal Court
- Appeal Court
- Supreme Court

The Irish Court system was established under Articles 64 to 73 of the Irish Constitution enacted in 1922. The Courts of Justice Act 1924 set out the structure and Hierarchy of the Irish Courts and the final structure of the Irish Courts was set out in the Irish Constitution of 1937 under Articles 34 to 38, there was a Constitutional challenge to the structure and hierarch of the Court set out in the 1937 Constitution, this challenge case "The State (Killian) v Minister for Justice [1954]" [49]found that new legislation was required to re-establish the hierarchy and structure of the Courts. This legislation came in the form of the Courts (Establishment and Constitution) Act 1961 and the Courts (Supplemental Provisions) Act 1961.

Article 34 of the Irish Constitution states that: "Justice shall be administered in courts established by law by Judges appointed in the manner provided by this Constitution"55 "justice will be administered by courts established by law and justice should generally be administered in public". This does not cover family law

Article 38 of the Irish Constitution states that 'no person shall be tried on any criminal charge save in the due course of law'.

The Irish Court system is hierarchical in nature with the Supreme Court being the highest, followed by the High Court, the Circuit Court, and the District Court. The Employment Appeals Tribunal, An Bord Pleanála, and the Labour Court are in the administrative divisions and deal with specialised areas of the law.

The superiority of Supreme Court judges was set out in the Courts of Justice Act 1924 and confirmed by the Courts Act 1997.

---

[49] The State (Killian) v Minister for Justice [1954] IR 207

55http://www.supremecourt.ie/supremecourt/sclibrary3.nsf/pagecurrent/D5F78352A38
7D74480257315005A419E?opendocument&l=en

The District Court

THE STRUCTURE OF IRISH COURTS

There are other administrative courts such as the Employment Appeals Tribunal, An Bord Pleanála, and the Labour Court inside the court hierarchy and structure.

The Courts and Court Officers (Amendment) Act 2007 states the numbers of judges in the District Court, 63, Circuit, 37, High 37, Special, 11 (from a panel), 3, 5 or 7 in the Supreme Court

Supreme Court

Final Court of Appeal (in cases of Fact only) only hears appeals, this court is not a court of first instance, (it never hears a case for the first time). It deals with matters of law or procedure where it's of national interest for the country such as the constitutionality of any legislation which may be referred under Article 26 of the constitution. The Supreme Court can determine or question capacity of the President. Three (ordinarily) or five (national importance) or 7 (Article 26) judges sit. Decisions made based on majority ruling, although each judge is eligible to provide a separate judgement, whether or not it agrees with majority rulings.

Court of Criminal Appeal

This court deals with appeals, persons convicted on impeachment in Circuit Court, Central Criminal Court or Special Criminal Court.

Special Criminal Court

This court deals with criminal charges relating to terrorist organizations and organized drug activities. Brought into being to secure effective administration of justice, preservation of public peace. It consists of three judges sitting without a jury. Set up under the *Offences against the State Act 1939*

Central Criminal Court

The Central Criminal Court is the criminal section of the High Court. It deals with serious indictable offences,. these would include rape, murder, piracy and treason.

Court of Civil Appeal

Hears appeals from High Court except cases where Supreme Court permits appeals. Gives ruling on question of law acquiesced to it by Circuit Courts. It hears appeals from cases heard in High Court about whether or not a law is constitutional.

High Court

The High Court has *full original jurisdiction (it can hear any case from anywhere for any amount)* in authority to determine, all complications, whether law or fact, civil and criminal. It has the authority to determine the validity of any law which is referred to it from the president under Article 26 of the constitution. It also deals with separation and divorce cases.

Circuit Court

The Circuit Civil Court deals with cases from €15k to €75k (Contract) and €60k (Tort) it also deals with family law separations and divorce.

The circuit criminal court deals with indictable offences which are less serious, i. e. theft burglary, robbery, some less indictable offences can be tried summarily in the district court with permission from the accused. DPP and the Judge. In criminal cases the judge sits with a jury. This court can also hear appeals from the District Court

Jurisdiction means: what the court has the power to deal with. i.e. limited jurisdiction in the district courts (€15,000), local jurisdiction in the district civil court is when the defendant lives or where the tort or contract took place. original jurisdiction means a case from any area for any amount.

Commercial Court

Provides efficient, effective dispute resolution in commercial cases greater than €1 million. Disputes concern of large commercial properties. Appeals or application for judicial review of regulator decisions.

District Court

The district civil court deals with minor civil law cases, maintenance orders up to €150.00 minor tort cases, this judge has the jurisdiction to deal with cases up to €15,000 this can deal with appeals from employment tribunals.

The district criminal court deals with minor offences, and offences which will give minor fines, in the district court you the maximum fine is €1905 and you will get a maximum sentence of 12 months for one offence and 24 months for two or more offences. This court deals with summary offences (less serious). Judge, no jury.

A summary offence is a minor offence heard by a judge only. indictable is a more serious offence which is heard by judge and jury

Small Claims

Claims up to €2k are dealt with without the need for a solicitor. The District Court Registrar will process the claim s/he will try to reach a settlement if this is not possible it will be brought before the District Court.

An Introduction to the Irish Court System

The Irish Court system was established under Articles 64 to 73 of the Irish Constitution enacted in 1922. **The Courts of Justice Act 1924** set out the structure and the hierarchy of the Irish Courts and the final structure of the Irish Courts was set out in the Irish Constitution of 1937 under Articles 34 to 38, there was a Constitutional challenge to the structure and hierarchy of the Court set out in the 1937 Constitution, this challenge case *"The State (Killian) v Minister for Justice [1954]"*[50] found that new legislation was required to re-establish the hierarchy and structure of the Courts. This legislation came in the form of **the Courts (Establishment and Constitution) Act 1961 and the Courts (Supplemental Provisions) Act 1961.**

Article 34 of the Irish Constitution states that: *"Justice shall be administered in courts established by law by Judges appointed in the manner provided by this Constitution"*[51] *"justice will be administered by courts established by law and justice should generally be administered in public".* This does not cover family law

Article 38 of the Irish Constitution states that 'no person shall be tried on any criminal charge save in the due course of law'. The Irish Court system is hierarchical in nature with the Supreme Court being the highest, followed by the High Court, the Circuit Court, and the District Court. The Employment Appeals Tribunal. An Bord Pleanála, and the Labour Court are in the administrative divisions and deal with specialised areas of the law. The superiority of Supreme Court judges was set out in **the Courts of Justice Act 1924** and confirmed by **the Courts Act 1997.** The Hierarchy of the Courts, starting with the inferior courts are as follow:

---

[50] The State (Killian) v Minister for Justice [1954] IR 207

[51] http://www.supremecourt.ie/supremecourt/sclibrary3.nsf/pagecurrent/D5F78352A387D74480257315005A419E?opendocument&l=en

The District Court in Ireland

The District Court is the lowest court in the court system; the District Court was established in 1961. ***The Courts and Court Officers (Amendment) Act 2007*** the numbers of judges should not be more than 60, excluding the President of the Court, however this has since been extended to 63. The currently President is Judge Rosemary Horgan.

There are 24 Districts in Ireland, including the Dublin Metropolitan District, each with its own court being presided over by a judge sitting alone (*that is, one judge, and no jury*).

Function & Jurisdiction

The District Court hears civil and criminal which are relatively minor. The District Court hear cases which are Summary in nature

District Civil Court

In civil cases, its monetary jurisdiction is limited to €15,000, meaning that that is the maximum award a judge can make in respect of a civil case. These cases are usually in Contract or Tort. This Court has the jurisdiction to grant liquor and lottery and competition licences, and can hear certain family matters, including issues relating to maintenance, which is limited to €150 per week per child, and €500 per week in respect of a spouse, access and guardianship, and can grant Safety Orders and Barring Orders, issues pursuant to the Control of Dogs Acts, applications to have birth and marriage certificates amended and applications for noise reduction orders under the ***Environmental Protection Act 1992***.

District Criminal Court

In criminal matters, its jurisdiction is limited to cases which a judge sits alone, (*there is no jury*) the maximum penalty is 12 months' imprisonment for one offence or 24 months for two or more offences.

Again, the maximum penalty is 12 months' imprisonment for one offence or 24 months for two or more offences. Cases in the District Court are those that are non-jury trials of minor offences which include most road traffic offences, TV licensing offences, and parking fines, these are called Summary (*or less serious*) offences.

There are some Indictable (*more serious*, and must have a jury) cases that cannot be heard in the District Court, including, rape, treason, murder, aggravated sexual assault, and piracy, which can never be heard in the District Court and must be referred up to the Circuit Court or the Central Criminal Court.

In respect of offences, the District Court Judge will be presented with the Book of Evidence, the prosecution and defence will present their submissions, including bail applications, before deciding whether there is a sufficient case to answer. If so, the accused will then be sent forward for trial to the Circuit Court or the Central Criminal Court, depending on the severity of the offence.

Appeals

There are, essentially, two types of appeal: a *de novo* appeal, and an appeal on a point of law.

De novo

When a *de novo* appeal is granted it means that the case is completely re-heard from the beginning by a higher court. For District Court cases, all *de novo* appeals are heard by the Circuit Court. The Circuit Court's determination is final and cannot be appealed.

On a point of law

 These are heard by the High Court, and can occur either during the case (referred to as a *"consultative case stated"*) or after the case has been heard in full (referred to as *"an appeal by way of case stated"*). In such appeals, the High

Court is only concerned with the legal issues and not in the findings of the District Court.

An example of this would be where there was some confusion as to the meaning of a particular law (*legislation*). If this was the case, the matter could be sent to the High Court to clear up any ambiguity. Once the matter is cleared up it is sent back to the District Court so that the case may continue, or so that any relevant changes can be made to the ruling.

Judicial review

While not strictly an appeal, there is also a remedy called **_judicial review._** In the District Court, this means that, where an individual is of the belief that a judge or other government agency has acted in excess of its jurisdiction (**_Ultra Virus,_** *acting outside the powers conferred on them*) or contrary to its duty, that person can query or challenge that action in the High Court.

The Small Claims Court

The small claims court deals mainly with minor matters. It provides consumers with an inexpensive and fast way to resolve disputes. This court is dealt with through the District Court offices. The Maximum claim that can be brought in the Small Claims court is €2.000 and normally deals with consumer matters and occasional small business complaints. Consumer claims such as faulty goods or bad workmanship are the normal type of consumer cases brought by persons in the small claims court. To be a consumer the customer must have bought the goods or engaged the service for private use from someone who sells them in the course of business.

A customer may also claim for the non-return of a rent deposit for some kinds of rented properties, such as a holiday home but excluded are deposit claims for private residential accommodation. Claims cannot be made in the Small Claims Court for debts, personal injuries or breach of leasing or hire-purchase agreements. The procedure for making a claim is commenced by lodging the claim with the District Court Registrar, and paying the fee of €25.00. The other party (*respondent or the person being claimed against*) will then be notified by the registrar of the District Court. If the Respondent does not agree with the claim they can dispute it by giving notice to the Registrar who will attempt to settle the claim, failing this case is set down for hearing. The case will be heard by a District Court Judge.

The parties can appeal the decision in the case to the Circuit Court within 14 days of the court hearing. If the decision is being appealed, the parties should consider obtaining legal advice.

The Circuit Court in Ireland

Under *the Court and Court Officers (Amendment) Act 2007* the Circuit Court comprises of 37 ordinary judges and is presided over by Mr. Justice Raymond Groarke.[52].

There are 8 Circuits in Ireland – Dublin, Cork, Eastern, South Eastern, Western, South Western, Northern, and Midlands. Dublin and Cork are the only permanent courts throughout the year.

 There are 10 judges assigned to the Dublin Circuit Court, and 3 to the Cork Circuit Court, the rest is divided between the remaining Circuit Courts. It also acts as an appeal court from the District Court. In criminal cases the Circuit Court is presided over by a judge sitting with a jury of twelve persons. In civil cases the Court is presided over by a judge sitting alone.

Function & Jurisdiction of the Circuit Court

The Circuit Court hears civil and criminal cases in a variety of matters which also include de novo appeals from the District Court. The Circuit Court covers indictable offences and has a jury

Structure of the Circuit Civil Court

The monetary jurisdiction in the Circuit Court is currently limited to where the claim does not exceed €75,000.00 and cases where the claim does not exceed €60,000 in personal injury, this means that that is the maximum monetary award that a judge can award when hearing a civil case. The Circuit Court deals with all breach of contract, property damage cases, family law i.e. judicial separation, divorce, nullity, and all ancillary matters i.e. family law matters which

---

[52] Circuit Court, County Registrar's duties and Responsibilities
The Registrar is also responsible for Motions of Discovery or issues arising in the service of documents.

can have secondary awards such as property division, land division, legal fees etc.

Structure of the Circuit Criminal Court

The Circuit Court has a wide jurisdiction in respect of criminal matters. It deals with all indictable offences which are sent forward from the District Court, however there are some exceptions, including rape, murder, aggravated sexual assault, treason, and piracy. These cases must be heard in the Central Criminal Court.

Appeals

Apart from hearing appeals from the District Court, the Circuit Court can also hear appeals from decisions of the Labour Court, the Unfair Dismissals Tribunal, and the Employment Appeals Tribunal. There are in essentially two types of appeal available to those whose judgements are in the Circuit Court: a *de novo* appeal, and an appeal on a point of law.

De novo

When a *de novo* appeal is granted it means that the case is completely re-heard from the beginning by a higher court. For District Court cases, all *de novo* appeals are heard by the High Court. For criminal cases, all *de novo* appeals are heard by the Court of Criminal Appeal. Determinations of the High Court and the Court of Criminal Appeal are final and cannot be appealed.

On a point of law

These are heard by the High Court, and can occur either during the case (*referred to as a "consultative case stated"*) or after the case has been heard in full (*referred to as "an appeal by way of case stated"*). In such appeals, the High Court is only concerned with the legal issues and not in the findings of the Circuit Court. An example of this would be where there was some confusion as to the meaning of a particular law (*legislation*). If this was the case, the matter could be sent to the High Court to clear up any ambiguity. Once the matter is cleared up it is sent back to the Circuit Court so that the case may continue, or so that any relevant changes can be made to the ruling.

Judicial review

While not strictly an appeal, there is also a remedy called ***judicial review.*** In the Circuit Court, this means that, where an individual is of the belief that a judge or other government agency has acted in excess of its jurisdiction (***Ultra Virus***) or contrary to its duty, that person can query or challenge that action in the High Court.

The High Court in Ireland

The High Court of Ireland has full original jurisdiction the power "to determine all matters and questions whether of law or fact, civil or criminal". It can decide the validity of any law, having regard to the provisions of the Constitution and hear murder and rape trials, through the **Competition Act, 2002** and associated cases or cases that result from it.[53]

Structure of the High Court of Ireland

The High Court is presided over by the Honourable Mr. Justice Nicholas Kearns and 36 ordinary judges. In Civil cases, one judge sitting alone usually presides over the proceedings, but in some cases of defamation, assault and battery, false imprisonment, and malicious prosecution all require a jury. There are times for instance, when there is a case of national importance i.e. the constitutionality of a new bill, the High Court will sit with three judges. The High Court hears appeals from the Circuit Court in civil cases. There are no juries per se in civil cases in the High Court with one exception; this exception is in libel cases where the case will be decided by a judge and jury. The High Court is based in Dublin but a division of the High Court sits in several provincial locations such as Cork, Galway, Limerick, Waterford, Sligo, Dundalk, Kilkenny and Ennis at specified times during the year to deal with personal injury cases and appeals from the various Circuit Courts in civil and family law matters.

Function & Jurisdiction of the High Court of Ireland

The High Court has full original jurisdiction, there is no local or limited jurisdiction. It can hear any cases for any amounts.

---

[53] Master of the High Court. The administrator of the High Court is the Master, their role is similar to that of the County Registrar of the Circuit Court, in that he is authorised to deal with various administrative matters in civil cases.

The High Court also hears de novo appeals from the Circuit Court in civil matters and appeals on a point of law from the District Court.

Structure of the High Court of Ireland

The High Court of Ireland also hears a variety of commercial issues, including applications to wind up a company, and bankruptcy matters. Other common types of cases to come before the High Court include personal injuries, defamation, and contract cases. Further, the High Court can hear judicial review applications in respect of government bodies, various tribunals, and even the decisions of lower courts. On the whole, although the High Court can hear any case as it has original jurisdiction claims of over €75,000 *(€60,000 in personal injury)* are usually dealt with in the High court, this has to do with practicalities and costs.

Structure of the High Court (Central Criminal Court) of Ireland

Where criminal matters are concerned, the High Court is referred to as the Central Criminal Court, or the Criminal Court area of the High Court. This court only hears cases of a more serious nature which the lower courts cannot deal with lower courts. Examples include murder, rape, aggravated sexual assault, treason, and piracy.

Appeals in the High Court of Ireland

An appeal from the High Court in civil cases can only go to the Supreme Court on foot of permission which is applied for under the "leapfrog appeal" system, however all other appeals go to the Court of Appeal...

The Special Criminal Court in Ireland

The Special Criminal Court was set up under ***the Offences against the State Act 1939*** and sits with no jury. The cases it can deal with are limited and usually Terrorism or Gangland. There is no Jury in this court and is presided over by three judges, these three judges are taken from a pool of 11 judges which are chosen from the High, Circuit and District Courts. Appeals from the Special Criminal Court against conviction or sentence are taken to the Court of Appeal.

The Court of Appeal in Ireland

The Court of Appeal, came into existence on 28th October 2014, it was established by the **Court of Appeal Act 2014,** the Court of Appeal which sits between the High Court and the Supreme Court.

The Court of Appeal is composed of a President and nine ordinary judges. The Chief Justice and the President of the High Court (The Honourable Mr Justice Sean Ryan) in addition to the President, the Court will comprise nine ordinary judges. Six High Court judges have been nominated for appointment to the Court, namely Mr Justice Peter Kelly, Ms Justice Mary Finlay Geoghegan, Mr Justice George Birmingham, Ms Justice Mary Irvine, Mr Justice Gerard Hogan, and, Mr Justice Michael Peart. The remaining three positions have yet to be filled by the Judicial Appointments Advisory Board. Some interlocutory and procedural applications may be heard by the President alone or by another judge nominated by the President. The Court of Appeal will be an automatic appeal court from the High Court.

Appeals in civil proceedings

The Court has jurisdiction to hear appeals in civil proceedings from the High Court which would have been heard by the Supreme Court prior to the introduction of the Court of Civil Appeal. It is possible to bypass the Court of Appeal or 'Leap Frog' an appeal to the Supreme Court., however permission from the Supreme Court to bring a Leapfrog Appeal must be obtained, this is not an automatic entitlement and will only be granted if the Supreme Court is satisfied that (i) the High Court decision involves a matter of general public importance; and/or (ii) the interests of justice require that the appeal be heard by the Supreme Court.[54] The Court can hear appeals from cases heard in the High Court about whether or not a law is constitutional. The Constitution provides that no laws may be passed restricting the Court of Appeal's jurisdiction to do this.

---

[54]   http://www.arthurcox.com/wp-content/uploads/2014/09/Arthur-Cox-Irelands-New-Court-of-Appeal-September-2014.pdf

Appeals in criminal proceedings

Under *the Court of Appeal Act 2014*, the Court of Appeal was given the appellate jurisdiction previously exercised by the Court of Criminal Appeal.

Criminal Appeals from the Circuit Court or Central Criminal Court who require a certificate from the trial judge that the case is a fit one for appeal now lie to the Court of Appeal. If this certificate is refused, the Court of Appeal itself, on appeal from this refusal, can grant leave to appeal. In addition, the Director of Public Prosecutions may appeal a sentence on grounds of alleged undue leniency under section 2 of the *Criminal Justice Act 1993*. An alleged case under miscarriage of justice, an appeal can be lodged under section 2 of the *Criminal Procedure Act 1993*. [55] The Court of Appeal was also given jurisdiction to hear appeals by the Director of Public Prosecutions on a question of law arising out of criminal trials which resulted in an acquittal. The decision of the Court of Appeal does not affect the acquittal verdict in such cases. Appeals by the Director of Public Prosecutions against an acquittal or against a decision not to order a retrial also lie to the Court of Appeal.

Courts-Martial appeals

Under the *Court of Appeal Act 2014*, the Court of Appeal was given the appellate jurisdiction previously exercised by the Courts-Martial Appeal Court. This means that appeals from people who have been convicted by a court-martial now lie to the Court of Appeal.

Cases stated

Questions of law which could previously be referred by the Circuit Court to the Supreme Court for determination (a 'case stated') are now determinable by the Court of Appeal.

---

[55]http://www.courts.ie/Courts.ie/library3.nsf/pagecurrent/5E9C21E72309A7D280257D7F0045A86A?opendocument

The Supreme Court

Appealing decisions of the Court of Appeal

Unless under very limited circumstances all decisions in the Court of Appeal are final, except in the following limited circumstances whereby permission can be sought from the Supreme Court to hear an appeal under **Article 34.5.3 of the Constitution** where:

(i)   the decision of the Court of Appeal involves a matter of general public importance;

    and/ or

(ii)   (ii) the interests of justice require that a further appeal be heard by it.

The Supreme Court in Ireland

The Supreme Court sits in the Four Courts in Dublin and is the highest court in the Irish legal system. It consists of the President or the Chief Justice, her Honour Ms. Justice Susan Denham and 7 ordinary judges. Under **section.5 of the Courts (No. 2) Act 1997**, the number of judges may also be exceeded by one where a former Chief Justice serves as a judge of the Supreme Court. The Court hears appeals from the High Court and the Court of Appeal. The Court has the power to decide if the provisions of any statute are repugnant to the Constitution should the President refer such provisions to the Court prior to the statute being enacted.

Under **Article 26 of the Irish Constitution 1937** the President has the power to send a Bill to the Supreme Court to test its constitutionality before signing it into law. In procedural matters or minor cases, three judges sit. For matters involving a constitutional challenge to a statute, or where an important question of law arises, five judge's sit, the Supreme Court can be requested to review a Bill referred to it by the President as to whether or not such a Bill is repugnant to the Constitution, if this event takes place then seven judges sit. Where there are applications for the appointment of Notaries Public and Commissioners for Oaths, or for case management lists the Chief Justice can sit alone.

Appeals

The main day-to-day business of the Supreme Court is to hear appeals from the Court of Appeal, or from the High Court ("leapfrog" appeals under limited circumstances "see high court notes"). The Supreme Court does not hear the evidence of witnesses as there is no witness box in the Supreme Court. Appeals are heard on the basis of the documents that were before the original court and a transcript of the oral evidence that was given in the original court and, where the trial judge approves them, legal counsels' notes of the evidence.

Decisions of Judges in the Supreme Court

Decisions are made based on a majority ruling, though each judge is entitled to deliver a separate judgement, regardless of whether or not it agrees with the majority ruling. There are two exceptions to this – where deciding on the validity of a law or on the constitutionality or otherwise of a Bill, the majority decision is the only one pronounced.

These decisions are sometimes given ex tempore (immediately). There are times however, when Judges reserve the right to reserve its decision pending consideration of the facts whereby they will deliver their decision at a future date.

Personnel in the Courts

Personnel involved in the court room

The Judge

 The judge is in charge of court proceedings and decides any legal issues arising in the case.

Points to Note

- A group of judges sitting together on a legal matter in the Court constitutes a bench.
- A division bench comprises of two or three judges.
- A constitutional bench comprises of five or more judges and may even extend to nine judges

The Registrar / Court Clerk

The registrar / court clerk assists the judge with administrative matters and is in charge of the court documents and exhibits. He/she also records the names of witnesses and the decision in the case. The registrar / court clerk also administers the oath.

Solicitor

Solicitors meet with clients and get instructions from them. They prepare the case for trial by getting the papers ready and choosing/briefing a barrister to present the case.

The Jury

 The jury hears the evidence and decides on the guilt or innocence of the accused in a criminal case and which party wins in a civil case.

Personnel in the Courts

The Court Reporter / Stenographer

The stenographer takes a note of everything said in the case and later types up the notes in the event of an appeal being lodged.

Witness

Witnesses are called by either party to prove their side of the story and may be cross-examined by the opposing party as to the accuracy of their evidence.

Counsel

The barristers in the case are known as counsel. They are hired by the solicitor to prosecute or defend the case in court. The barristers constitute the members at the bar.

DPP (criminal)

The Department of public prosecutions brings cases against the accused in criminal cases; they bring the case on behalf of the citizens.

Tipstaff / Judge's Usher

The tipstaff / judge's usher is the personal assistant to the judge. He/she walks ahead of the judge carrying a staff and says "all rise" as the judge enters the courtroom.

Defendant (criminal)

The accused comes before the court accused of a crime.

 ### Defendant (civil)

The person being sued or the case is being brought against.

Plaintiff

This is the person bringing the civil case against another civilian or the state.

Prison Officer (Criminal)

They sit in attendance with the accused.

Public

Members of the general public are permitted in the public gallery, except in camera or family/child custody cases.

The Differences between a solicitor and a barrister in Irish law

- Barristers present legal cases in Court before Judges and Juries as well as give their opinions on questions of law.
- Barristers in Ireland can only act when a solicitor briefs them on a case. They cannot simply turn up in Court and have a right of audience (advocate on behalf of anyone)
- A Solicitor will deal with the client and prepare the case for the barrister to present. (as they have specialised knowledge in that specific area)
- Solicitors can advertise. Barristers cannot.
- Solicitors can form firms, Barristers can come together with other barristers under one roof called a chambers,
- Barristers are self-employed. Solicitors are not. They are employed or partners in firms.
- Barristers in the same chamber can work opposing cases, solicitors in the same firm cannot represent two side of a dispute, and this is conflict of interest.

- Solicitors deal directly with the public and contracted to them; barristers are contracted to the solicitor.
- Barristers specialise in set areas of law, solicitors are knowledgeable in many broad areas of law.
- Solicitors Qualify with the Law Society of Ireland and Barristers qualify with the King's Inn.
- Barristers AND solicitors can become judges.

Suing a Solicitor or Barrister

It is possible to sue a solicitor for breach of contract as there is a contract between solicitor and client. However, there is **no such contract between a client and barrister.** It is possible to sue a solicitor or a barrister for negligence in and out of court.

Civil Liability & Courts Act 2004

Many people involved in claims believe that over time this act has an even greater chance of revolutionising the overall scene. While no one has objection to reasonable compensation being paid to genuine claimants by those who are liable for their injuries, far too often many of these vital components were ignored. Added to this was the requirement to pay costs in far too many straightforward cases. PIAB is really more about that problem; The Courts Act begins to get to the heart of the matter.

Criminal Law

In Ireland, there are approx. 670 crimes committed every day, and alarmingly those do not include motoring offences (central statistics office), with theft accounting for over 30% of those crimes. Criminal law is mainly aimed at controlling behaviours within society.

The purpose of this introductory booklet is to provide readers with a outline understanding of the principles of criminal law in Ireland and to enable them to appreciate the role of criminal law in their personal and vocational lives. It is also intended to prepare readers for their personal lives or further study in related areas.

Readers who complete this booklet will:

- develop a general understanding of the Irish Criminal System
- develop an appreciation of the elements required for a crime to be committed
- evaluate the impact of relevant legislation governing the various aspects of criminal law to be investigated
- acquire skills in evaluation and analysis
- be familiar with the language and procedures related to the various aspects of criminal law studied.

Criminal law in Ireland

The Main Elements of a Crime

Most crimes comprise two elements, an Actus Reus ("*guilty act*") and a Mens Rea ("*guilty mind*").

Actus non facitreum nisi mens sit rea. Correctly translated, this means "***An act does not make a man guilty of a crime, unless his mind be also guilty***."

Therefore, it is not the actus which is "reus" but the man and his mind separately. All crimes require proof of an Actus Reus.

Also, there is a presumption that each part of the Actus Reus requires proof of a corresponding Mens Rea. Offences to which the presumption of Mens Rea does not apply are called crimes of strict liability.

(**Example**: *Strict liability means that no intention on behalf of the wrongdoer is needed, such as motoring offences, drink-driving, speeding etc, therefore prosecution need not prove you intended to speed to convict you of speeding contrary to the Road Traffic Act.*)

Actus Reus

> *Actus Reus of an offence consists of:*
> *1) a voluntary*
> *2) act*
> *3) that causes*
> *4) social harm.*

"The Guilty Act". An Actus Reus always includes <u>conduct</u> (*behaviour*) on the part of the *Defendant* (<u>*suspect*</u>). It may also include a particular circumstance (*things that happened* or actions which the suspect performed), and/or a particular <u>result</u> caused by the suspect's conduct. *Supposing "A" shoots and kills an on-duty member of the Garda Siochana and is consequently charged with murder under* **s 3 of the Criminal Justice Act 1990**. In order to secure a conviction, the prosecution would have to prove, inter alia (*amongst other things*), the following Actus Reus:

1. The act of shooting (*conduct*),
2. That the victim was an on-duty member of An Garda Siochana(*circumstance*), and
3. The death of the victim (*result*).

There is no legal punishment for mere thoughts, and no person can be prosecuted for thinking bad thoughts.

Criminal law in Ireland

Mens Rea

"The Guilty Mind". As a general rule, each part of an Actus Reus (*conduct, circumstance and result*) requires proof of a corresponding Mens Rea (*guilty mind*) on the part of the offender. If at least one part of an Actus Reus does not require proof of a corresponding Mens Rea on the part of the suspect, the offence is one of strict liability. The prosecution (DPP) must prove that the suspect had intended the conduct.

Let us return to our example of "A" shooting and killing an on-duty member of An Garda Siochana and being charged with murder contrary to **s 3 of the Criminal Justice Act 1990.** To secure "A's conviction, the Prosecution would have to prove, inter alia, (*amongst other things*) the following Actus Reus:

- That A shot the victim (*conduct*),
- That the victim was an on-duty member of An Garda Siochana (*circumstance*), and
- That the death of the victim (*result*) was caused by A's conducted.

Each part of this _Actus Reus_ requires proof of a corresponding _Mens Rea_. So, it would have to be proved that A's conduct was _deliberate_ or _voluntary_. If **A** shot the victim whilst sleepwalking, he would be entitled to an acquittal on the ground of automatism. In addition, it would have to be proved that **A** either _knew of the circumstance or was reckless as to its existence, i.e. that he knew the victim was on on-duty Garda, or was reckless as to whether or not the victim was an on-duty member of An Garda Siochana._ Finally, it would have to be proved that **A** _intended to kill or to cause serious injury to some person, whether the person actually killed or not._

Intention

In People **(DPP) v Douglas and Hayes (1985)** the Court of Criminal Appeal considered the meaning of "intention" in the context of **s 14 of the Offences Against the Person Act 1861**, which provides, _"whosoever shall shoot at any person with intent to commit murder, shall, whether any bodily injury be effected or not, be guilty of a felony"_

The applicants had been convicted in the Special Criminal Court of; inter alia, an offence contrary to s. *14 of the 1861 Act.* They succeeded in arguing that the intent required by s. 14 had not been proved. **McWilliam J** delivered the judgment of the court, saying, "*Unless the suspect has actually expressed intent,* *his intent can only be ascertained from a consideration of his actions and the surrounding circumstances."*

*(**Example**: In order for a person to be guilty of theft they must take an item of property belonging to another person (guilty act), they must also intend (guilty mind) that they deprive that person of it and keep it for themselves).*

What then is the difference between criminal law and civil law?.

***Criminal law** – This is the punishment of wrongdoers by the state (maintaining social order)*

***Civil law** – This deals with the compensation of losses; system of rights and remedies for regulating interaction between members of society.*

Criminal law in Ireland

What is Criminal Law?

Criminal law governs crimes. Crimes are generally referred to as offences against the state. It is an offence against the community at large, not an individual. The standard of proof for crimes is "*beyond a reasonable doubt.*" A crime is defined in law in Ireland as an act which may be punished by the State. The way in which a criminal offence is investigated and prosecuted depends on the type of crime involved. For this purpose criminal offences may be described in different ways such as:

- Summary offences
- Indictable offences
- Minor offences
- Serious offences
- Arrestable offences

There are two ways criminal offences can be tried in Irish law:

- In the lower (minor) court (District Court) before a judge **without** a jury (summary).

- In the higher (major) courts (Circuit Criminal Court, Central Criminal Court) before a judge and jury (indictable).

Article 38 of the constitution of Ireland provides:

1. No person shall be tried on any criminal charge save in due course of law
2. Minor offences may be tried by courts of summary jurisdiction
3. Save in the case of trial of offences under section 2, no person shall be tried on any criminal charge without a jury

This constitutional article determines that unless a matter is summary (not very serious, i.e. TV licence, parking, speeding, car tax, etc.) then it must be dealt with before a judge and jury.

Article 40 of the constitution of Ireland

Section 3, Subsection 1(1) The State guarantees in its laws to respect, and, as far as practicable, by its laws to defend and vindicate the personal rights of the citizen.

Criminal law in Ireland

Subsection (1) the State only guarantees to "respect, and, as far as practicable, by its laws defend and vindicate the personal rights of the citizen." In today's society it can be asked, is ***as far as practicable*** enough to ensure the State protects its citizens.

Section3. Subsection (2) The State shall, in particular, by its laws protect as best it may from unjust attack and, in the case of injustice done; vindicate the life, person, good name, and property rights of every citizen.

Subsection (2) refers only to one set of rights, namely the property rights of every citizen. What it undertakes to protect (against unjust attack) and vindicate (in the case of injustice done) are simply every citizen's life, person and good name, not the right to life, the right to good name.

These are just a few of the essential elements for a crime, you can have a full breakdown of criminal law in my Introduction to Criminal Law book.

The lighter side of the law

The lighter side of the law

Not everything about the law needs to be staunch and boring, in fact the law is exciting, dynamic and interesting, its can however be difficult sometimes to find humour or fun when you are trying to get to grips with the doctrines, rules and principles.

I will finish off this booklet on a lighter note, a selection of Irish laws and of course International ones too, so that you can see the lighter side of the law before you close the book. Enjoy and have a giggle, or even awe (maybe)

Ireland has its fair share of strange and (by modern standards) weird laws.

Plain Weird Laws in Ireland

1.   It is illegal to perform witchcraft in Ireland: Any person who shall pretend or exercise to use any type of witchcraft, sorcery, enchantment, or pretend knowledge in any occult or craft or science shall for any such offense suffer imprisonment at the time of one whole year and also shall be obliged to obscursion (not seen) for his/her good behaviour.

2:      It is illegal for a student to walk through Trinity College without a sword.

3:      In Trinity college students can demand a glass of brandy at any time during an exam, provided they are wearing their sword and hand it up.

4.   It is illegal to be drunk in a pub, (it is illegal for landlords to continue to serve alcohol to an intoxicated person)

5.   It is illegal to smoke tobacco on Grafton Street.

6.   If a Leprechaun calls at your door you must, by law, give him a share of your dinner.

7.   Holders of the freedom of Dublin have the right to pasture sheep on common ground within the city boundaries. (Remember Bono and the sheep grazing in Dublin?). However, some say that by doing so they accidentally

broke the law at the same time as you are only allowed to graze your own sheep, not borrowed ones.

8.   *The Tippling Act 1735* prohibits a publican from pursuing a customer for money owed for any drink given on credit. (How many slates are illegally followed?)

9.   (Any aspiring Sheldon's beware). It is illegal to conduct nuclear tests in the city. This law from 2006 clearly states that: "A person who carries out, or causes the carrying out of, a nuclear explosion in the State shall be guilty of an offense."

10.   Crossing a railway track on a bicycle is illegal whereas you can drive across it legally. You are still supposed to dismount and walk your bike across at a level crossing.

And Whacky Laws

1.   You can shoot someone and kill them from the top of the campinile (bell tower) in Trinity College, on a particular day of the year and not be charged with murder. However, it is impossible to find out what day of the year it is....

2.   Law: It is illegal to operate a flashing amber beacon on an agricultural tractor (and many other vehicles).

Repealed Laws

3.   Henry VIII declared that: a pilot of a ship who runs aground in Dublin Bay will be blinded as punishment for their incompetence.

4.   The penalty for suicide was death by hanging. [56])

---

[56] (http://www.staycity.com/category-dublin/15-unbelievable-laws-in-dublin-you-might-have-to-adhere-to-while-in-the-city/

The lighter side of the law

Some newspaper excepts from Irish cases

Humour in court can heal drugs pain - Anne-Marie Walsh

May 5 2006 12:11 AM

COMEDIAN Des Bishop dispensed words of wisdom from the judge's bench yesterday as two men graduated with honours in the difficult subject of ditching drugs.

The Corkman kept the court in stitches as he praised the efforts made by the latest Drugs Treatment Court success stories - a 23-year-old with a cocaine addiction and a 32-year-old heroin addict who have come through two of the most gruelling years of their lives.

Both men, who did not want to be named, are part of a pioneering system of drugs rehab that rewards participants by dropping charges against them as they progress.

As they go through months of 'cold turkey' that includes regular urine tests, schooling and counselling, they gradually whittle down their charges to zero.

The outcome is the unfamiliar sight of a happy courtroom where the perpetrators of crime are applauded as they are rewarded by a judge.

Judge Bridget Reilly also promised a 'surprise' in the shape of comedian Des Bishop. The room was in stitches when he joked "I could get ?5 for that".[57]

---

[57] http://www.independent.ie/irish-news/humour-in-court-can-heal-drugs-pain-26383053.html

The lighter side of the law

I Got an Apology from the Barrister

Calmness is over and it's back to mayhem. I was actually in the High Court in Dublin last week as a witness in a case where basically a publican is trying to get a pub license. While one of the owners was in the witness box, the state's senior council said that the Cully and Sully pies were just fast food and the same as Cuisine De France - which I took serious exception to. I was then called into the witness box and asked to outline who our customers were so I told the Judge that our customers included Cleary's Tearooms restaurant, Bank Of Ireland and that actually we are about to start supplying the Four Courts at the request of some high court judges!!!!! I then turned around to the States Barrister and told her that "indeed we were not Cuisine De France". To which the entire court erupted in laughter and I got an apology from the barrister.

Brilliant: I then legged it out of the box!!!!!!!![58]

And...

Longford District Court Sitting – 2016 (my own)

Defendant: (an elderly man), was called to the stand, charged with speeding; the defendant slowly makes his way to the witness box...

Judge; you are charged; on x day 2016, you were found to be spe... Ring...Ring... defendant's mobile phone rings;

Defendant: judge, can I take this.... Judge; feel free ... defendant; I can't talk right now, I'm in court, (other party .....!) no I'm talking to the judge .....(Courtroom erupts in laughter)

---

[58] http://www.cullyandsully.com/content/i-got-apology-barrister[last accessed 2nd Mary 2017]

The lighter side of the law

Weird Laws in the United Kingdom

1. Since 1313, MPs are not allowed to don armour in Parliament.

2. No cows may be driven down the roadway between 10 AM and 7 PM unless there is prior approval from the Commissioner of Police.

3. All land must be left to the eldest son. (Not just the UK.... Huh)

4. Excluding Sundays, it is perfectly legal to shoot a Scotsman with a bow and arrow.

5. A bed may not be hung out of a window.

6. *It is legal for a male to urinate in public, as long it is on the rear wheel of his motor vehicle and his right hand is on the vehicle.*

7. A license is required to keep a lunatic.

8. It is illegal for a lady to eat chocolates on a public conveyance.

9. Committing suicide is classified as a capital crime.

10. With the exception of carrots, most goods may not be sold on Sunday.

11. It is illegal to shoot a Welshman with a crossbow on Thursdays.

12. In Liverpool, it is illegal for a woman to be topless except as a clerk in a tropical fish store.

13. Any person found breaking a boiled egg at the sharp end will be sentenced to 24 hours in the village stocks (enacted by Edward VI).

The lighter side of the law

And of Course, Plain Crazy from the USA

1.   Bear wrestling matches are prohibited.

2.   Incestuous marriages are legal. (In Alabama)

3.   You may not have an ice cream cone in your back pocket at any time.

4.   It is considered an offense to open an umbrella on a street, for fear of spooking horses.

5.   Women are able to retain all property they owned prior to marriage in the case of divorce. However, this provision does not apply to men. (Interesting, and quite unfair)

6.   It is illegal to sell peanuts in Lee County after sundown on Wednesday.

7.   It is illegal for a driver to be blindfolded while operating a vehicle.

8.   It is illegal to wear a fake moustache that causes laughter in church.

9.   Putting salt on a railroad track may be punishable by death.

10.   Men who deflower virgins, regardless of age or marital status, may face up to five years in jail.

Conclusion

The definition of crime is challenging because acts that are defined as criminal vary across time and cultures. Many criminologists believe that because crimes are over defined they cannot determine what real crimes are and criminals are.

This introductory guide was designed to give you a background in Criminology, if you would like to continue your criminology studies further I recommend the following books and publications as part of your academic or personal learning journey into the study, causation, and prevention of crime.

References

Recommended reading

Carrabine, E., Iganski, P., Lee, M., Plummer, K. and South, N. (2008) Criminology: A Sociological Introduction. London: Routledge.

Hale et al. [2013 ed.] Criminology [3rd ed.]. Oxford: Oxford UP.

Kilkelly, U [2006] Youth Justice in Ireland: Tough Lives, Rough justice. Sallins, Co. Kildare: Irish Academic Press.

Kilcommins, S[2004] Crime, punishment and the search for order in Ireland. Dublin: Institute of Public Administration.

Maguire, M. (ed) (2012) The Oxford Handbook of Criminology. Oxford: Oxford University Press

McLaughlin & John Muncie [2013] The Sage Dictionary of Criminology. [3rd ed.]. London: Sage.

Webber, C. (2010) Psychology and Crime. London: Sage

References

Bibliography

Bonger et al (1916) Criminality and economic conditions, Little, Brown, and Company, Boston

Briggs J. Harrison C. McInnes A. Vincent D. (2005) Crime and Punishment in England: An introductory History London: Routledge

Burke R.H. (2005) An Introduction to Criminal Theory Cullompton: Willan Publishing

Chesney-Lind, M., & Irwin, K. (2004). From badness to meanness: Popular constructions of contemporary girlhood. In A. Harris (Ed.), All about the girl: Culture, power, and identity (pp. 45–56). New York: Routledge.

Citizens Information. (2014). Supreme Court of Ireland. Retrieved May 2014, from Citizen Information: http://www.citizensinformation.ie/en/justice/courts_system/supreme_court.ht ml

Clarke, R. V. and M. Felson (Eds.) (1993). Routine Activity and Rational Choice. Advances in Criminological Theory, Vol 5. New Brunswick, NJ: Transaction Books. Cockburn J. S. (1977) Crime in England 1550-1800 London: Methuen & Co Ltd.

Clyne T. (2016) The Irish Legal System. First Edition . Createspace. New york

Courts Service. (2009). History of the state. Retrieved from Courts Service: http://www.courts.ie/Courts.ie/library3.nsf/pagecurrent/8B9125171CFBA7808 0256DE5004011F8?opendocument

Cunneen, C. and White, R. (2007) Juvenile Justice: Youth and Crime In Australia, Third Edition, Oxford University Press, Melbourne.

Department of Justice, Equality and Law Reform (2009) Fear of Crime in Ireland and its Impact on Quality of Life. Stationary Office. Dublin

Evans E.J. (1994) Sir Robert Peel London: Routledge.

References

Garland D. (1997) 'Of Crimes and Criminals: The Development of Criminology in Britain.

Graber, D. (1980). Crime News and the Public. New York: Praeger Publishers Hirschi, T (1969) Causes of Delinquency. University of California Press.

Irish Statute Book. (2009). Criminal Justice (Public Order) Act, 1994. Retrieved 2012, from Irish Statute Book, : http://www.irishstatutebook.ie/eli/1994/act/2/section/8/enacted/en/html

Irish Statute Book. (2009). Criminal Justice (Public Order) Act, 1994. Retrieved 2011, from Irish Statute Book: http://www.irishstatutebook.ie/eli/1994/act/2/section/9/enacted/en/html Irish Statute Book. (2010). Criminal Justice Act 2006. Retrieved 2012, from Irish Statute Book: http://www.irishstatutebook.ie/eli/2006/act/26/section/184/enacted/en/html Irish Statute

Book. (2014). Criminal Justice (Public Order) Act 2011. Retrieved 2014, from Irish Statute Book: http://www.irishstatutebook.ie/eli/2011/act/5/section/2/enacted/en/html Irish Statute

Book S14. (n.d.). Criminal Justice (Public Order) Act, 1994. Retrieved from Irish Statute Book: http://www.irishstatutebook.ie/eli/1994/act/2/section/14/enacted/en/html Irish Statute

Book S15. (2012). Section 15 of the Criminal Justice (Public Order) Act 1994 . Retrieved 2013, from Irish Statute Book: http://www.irishstatutebook.ie/eli/1994/act/2/section/15/enacted/en/html Irish Statute

Book S16. (2010). Criminal Justice (Public Order) Act, 1994. Retrieved 2012, from Irish Statute Book: http://www.irishstatutebook.ie/eli/1994/act/2/section/16/enacted/en/html

Irish Statute book, S. (2009). Criminal Justice Act (Public order) Act 1994. Retrieved 2011, from Irish Statute Book: http://www.irishstatutebook.ie/eli/1994/act/2/section/18/enacted/en/html Klein D.

References

(2004) The Etiology of Female Crime in McLaughlin E. Muncie J. Hughes G(Eds.) Criminological Perspectives (2nd Ed) London: Sage

Maguire M. Morgan R. Reiner R. (eds) The Oxford Handbook of Criminology Oxford: Oxford University Press.

McIntyre, McMullan and O Toghda, Criminal Law (Dublin, 2012) McAuley and McCutcheon, Criminal liability: A Grammar (Dublin, 2000).

Nelken D. (1997) 'White Collar Crime' in Maguire M. Morgan R. Reiner R. (eds) The Oxford Handbook of Criminology Oxford: Oxford University Press

NI Shuinear, S. (2003); 'Irish Travellers: 'Ethnolect, Alliance, Control', (London), University of Greenwich

Siegel, Larry J. (2006) Criminology; 9th Edition. Thomson/Wadsworth, Belmont, CA.

Skogan, W. (1987). 'The Impact of Victimisation on Fear'. Crime and Delinquency 33(1): 135-154

Soothill, K. Peelo, M. Taylor, C. (2003) Making Sense of Criminology. Cambridge: Polity

The Brehon Laws. (2011). Retrieved April 2014, from Brehon Law: http://brehonlaw-justice.blogspot.ie/2013/03/the-brehon-law.html

Tierney J. (2009) Perspectives in Criminology Maidenhead: Open University Press. Woods, Kieron (2011) The Irish Legal System [ONLINE] Last accessed 2 July 2012 http://irishbarrister.com/legalterms.html

Young, J. (1997), 'Left Realist Criminology: Radical in its Analysis, Realist in its Policy' in M. Maguire, R. Morgan & R. Reiner (eds), The Oxford Handbook of Criminology, Oxford: Oxford University Press

Printed in Great Britain
by Amazon

86581444R00136